Authority and Forms of Political Protest in Indian Tradition

Authority and Forms of Political Protest in Indian Tradition

Ashok S. Chousalkar

KALPAZ

First Published, 2017

Published by

Kalpaz Publications
C-30, Satyawati Nagar,
Delhi – 110052
E-mail: kalpaz@hotmail.com
Ph.: 9212142040

Printed at: G. Print Process, Delhi

Cataloging in Publication Data—DK
Courtesy: D.K. Agencies (P) Ltd. <docinfo@dkagencies.com>

Chousalkar, Ashok S., 1950- **author.**
Authority and forms of political protest in Indian tradition / by Ashok S. Chousalkar.
pages cm
Includes bibliographical references.
ISBN 9789386397065

1. Protest movements—India—History—To 1500. 2. India—Politics and government—To 997. 3. Authority. I. Title.

DS451.C46 2017 DDC 934 23

Contents

Preface

In Political theory there is a close relationship between nature of political authority and political obligation because obtaining regular obedience of the people, is the necessary condition for stability and security of the state. In ancient Indian texts there was considerable discussion on authority and forms of political protest. Notable among them are the *Mahabharata*, the *Jatakas*, the *Kathasaritsagar* and the *Rajtarangini* of Kalhan. In the turbulent history of Kashmir the people followed both non-violent and violent methods to oppose the wrong policies of the government. The Brahmins in Kashmir used to offer *dharana* and if their demands were not met, they took recourse to suicide.

The Indians believed that ultimately the mandate to rule was depended on the observance of principles of Dharma. Hence, Dharma formed the heart of political authority. Kalhan, in the *Rajtarangini* said that the *Kalpvriksha* delivered rewards when you desired but the tree of Dharma dispensed rewards without any demand. The Indian thinkers always held that the fearlessness was the essence of Dharma. The Mahabharata pointed out that one should not get scared of king; cheat and the wicked

Indian freedom fighters such as Lokmanya Tilak, Sri Aurobindo, Mahatma Gandhi and Bhagat Singh took recourse to different forms of political protest to fight against the British rule. Tilak, Aurobindo and Gandhi supported the theory of passive resistance but Sawarkar, Hardayal and Bhagat Singh followed the method of armed resistance. These leaders wanted to liberate their countrymen. In ancient India, the people first tried to use non-violent method to change the policy of the government and if the government continued to follow the same policies, the people finally took recourse to violent means including assassinations, mass uprisings and the armed conflict. Initially, they wanted to change the policy of the government but if the government did not do so they tried to change the government and new king was installed.

My daughter Rita took keen interest in the publication of the book and provided necessary inputs. This research work was financed by the University Grants Commission, New Delhi and I am thankful to UGC for the support. I am also thankful to Librarian of Shivaji University Library for giving me necessary help. I am specially thankful to Dr. Suryakant Gaikwad for giving me all sort of assistance including the typing of the manuscript. I have completed this work in the Department of Political Science of Shivaji University and I thank students, teachers and non-teaching staff for their support. I am deeply indebted to Kalpaz Publications, Delhi for agreeing to publish the book.

Ashok Chousalkar

Kolhapur

Chapter – I

Introduction

In Political Theory, the concept of political authority played an important role because authority is the expression of state power. The political authority has to be exercised with the consent of the people. Withdrawal of the consent causes erosion of authority. Therefore, constitution of political authority and forms of political protest are two interrelated themes, for, the lack of efficacy of political authority gave birth to different types of protests. In ancient Indian political thought, there is some discussion on the interrelationship between political authority and legitimacy (Chousalkar, (1976: 58-70).

Political Authority

As far as political authority is concerned, there are three different meanings which continue to interchange. Firstly, authority means the right of a particular person to rule and that right is established by traditional norms or by the basic law of the country. Secondly, it means recognition of that right by the governed. The governed recognise that right and obey the orders of the ruler without any problem. Thirdly, authority means the ability of the governing body to influence the behaviour of the governed through the method of ideological persuation. This enables authority to obtain regular obedience of the people. In ancient Greece, it is believed that the constitution shapes life and mental make up of the citizens according to its ideology. Therefore, the democratic constitution gave birth to democratic men. The Mahabharata also said that the king was the maker of the age in the sense that he shaped lives of the people.

Logic of Shankha and Likhita

In ancient Indian political thought the problem of political authority was resolved with the help of the concept of **Shankha-Likhita Nyaya** or the logic of Shankha-Likhita. A Smriti was known by their name. The story of Shankha and Likhita was narrated in the Mahabharata (12.24). Shankha and Likhita were two brothers living on the bank of Bahuda river in their separate houses. One day Likhita picked up some ripe fruits from the orchard of Shankha without taking his permission. When Shankha came to know about this, he told his brother that this was an act of theft and he should suffer punishment for the same. Likhita apologized and requested Shankha to punish him. He told him that it was not his right to punish him as only the king of the land had a right to punish him. Both of them went to the king. Initially the king was not ready to punish him but because of their insistence he punished Likhita by cutting off his hands. After this he went to take bath in the river, both of his hands were restored due to divine intervention.

The moral of story is clear. It is the authority of the king to punish the wrong doer. No one else has a right to punish a person for his crime. It is royal privilege.

Three Traditions

In ancient India, there existed three different political traditions : (1) the *arthashastra* tradition, (2) the Buddhist tradition and (3) the *dharmashastra – Smriti* tradition. All these three traditions recognised importance of political authority and they used social contract theory of origin of state to legitimise the authority of the state. In the *arthashastra* tradition, it is argued that the state arose to overcome the logic of fishes in the society. In the Buddhist tradition, the *Mahasammata* or Chief was elected to overcome anarchy as well as to provide protection to the people. This was useful tool to legitimize the authority of *gana-samgha* polity. (Thapar, 1979: 117-30) In the Smriti tradition, the state which had quasi-divine, quasi-contractual origin, arose to protect four-fold social order as well as to protect the people from anarchy. In all these traditions, it is said that kingship was created to protect people from anarchy and in liu of that the people agreed to pay taxes.

Authority and Dharma

In ancient India, authority was rooted in traditional sanctions and religion played an important role in it. The Vedic ritual of sacrifices was used to legitimise the authority of the king. Divinity and authority of the king was rooted in the performance of these sacrifices.

The king in ancient India would lose his legitimacy if he ceased to follow the law of Dharma. The king who lost control over his senses was bound to lose his control over the state. Hence Dr. Anand Coomaswami wrote, "Self-importance of the king leads to disintegration and finally the death of the body politic-collective or individual. The message of the traditional politics was that self-government (Swaraj) depended on self control" (Coomarswami, 1978: 85). It is believed that when the king lost self-control, he would invite the wrath of the people.

The people all over the world who were not happy with the king took recourse to different methods of protest and developed different forms of resistance. In India, also people took recourse to different methods of protest. Earlier, it was said by the Orientalist scholars that the Indians were passive people and even if they were ruled by evil tyrants and desperate despots, they would not take recourse to rebellion. It was said by Hegel that in the East only one man was free and rest of the population was slave. But now the progressive research had shown that this was not the case and in India also, the people took recourse to violent and non-violent protests to fight against the despots (Ruben, 1968: 111-18).

Resistance and Protest

In India, we have a long tradition of political resistance and protest. People came out openly against the government to resist its wrong policies. They wanted to achieve following goals by opposing the government.

(1) To request king and his government to change its wrong and oppressive policies.

(2) To pressurise king to replace his wicked and cunning ministers.

(3) To force king to abdicate his throne for his successor.

(4) To assassinate tyrannical king.

(5) To bring about change in the political system.

People followed different methods to bring about change in the policies of the king. They include submitting request, offering dharana, fast and fast unto death, committing suicide, assassination of wicked king or minister and mass revolt by the populace to replace the king. Sometimes help of the frontier chief or the neighbouring king is solicited to bring about polical change in the country.

In this book, I would like to deal with three important aspects of political theory- the problem of constitution of political authority in India, and the methods of its legitimisation, the problem of political resistance in ancient India in the light of various forms of protest that had been used by the people including the method of armed rebellion and thirdly, the methods of resolution of the discontent of the people in the Indian tradition. In the present work, an attempt is made to understand how Indian people sought to deal with these problems.

Objectives of the Study

Following are the objectives of the present research –

(1) To understand the nature of constitution of political authority in ancient India and to probe its bases.

(2) To study the role played by the Vedic sacrifices, consecration ceremony and the clergy in the legitimisation of political authority.

(3) To examine the meaning and nature of social contract theory of origin of state in the *arthashastra*, the Buddhist and the *Smriti* traditions and its impact on their political theory.

(4) To study various forms of protest and the methods of resistance used by the people in ancient India.

(5) To assess the effectiveness and contemporary relevance of ancient Indian methods of resolution of conflicts and reconciliation of discords.

Methodology

The present study is essentially a library-based research project as it has used different literary sources to gather necessary information. The main sources used are that of the Vedic literature that is mainly the *Rigveda* and the *Atharvaveda, Brahmanas* and *Upanishads*, the Nikay books and the *Jataka* stories, the *Mahabharata*, the *arthashastra* of Kautilya, the *Katha Sarit Sagar* of Somadeva and the *Rajatarangini* of Kalhana. Thus, the study covers period from 1500 B.C. to 1100 A.D. But the study is essentially based on above mentioned material. The approach of study is historical in the sense that it studies the process of constitution of political authority and strategies of legitimisation in the light of growth of social and economic forces in ancient India. It also studies the role of ideology in the formation of political authority as well as in emergence of different types of revolts and insurgencies in the state. It has pieced together different evidences that are spread over in different books in ancient India. Our evidences show us that since the Vedic period, Indian people devised different means of protest and revolt against the established political authority, if the same was not responsive to resolve their grievances.

In the subsequent Chapters, the topics like the constitution of political authority in ancient India, ideology and forms of protest in the Buddhist literature and in the Mahabharata, the problem of political rebellion in the *arthashastra* of Kautilya and the methods of and forms of protest used in the stories of the *Katha Sarit Sagar* and in the history of Kashmir which is graphically described in *Rajatarangini* of Kalhana- are elaborately discussed. In the last chapter, a critical analysis of political authority and forms of political protest used by the Indian people is made.

References

Chousalkar, A. (1976), "*Power, Authority and Legitimacy in Ancient India*", pp. 58-70, *Political Science Review.*

Coomarswami, Anand (1978), *The Spiritual Authority and the Temporal Power in the Indian Theory of Government*, Manshiram Manoharlal, Delhi.

Ruben, W. (1968), "*Fighting Against the Despots in Ancient India*", pp. 111-118, *Annals of Bhandarkar Oriental Research Institute,* Pune.

Thapar, R. (1979), "Ethics, Religion and Social Protest in First Millennium of Northern India", pp. 115-130 in *Dissent, Protest and Reform in Indian Civilisation*, edited by S. C. Malik, Indian Institute of Advanced Study, Shimla.

Chapter – II

Political Authority in Ancient India

In ancient India, there is considerable discussion on nature of political authority, the relations between power and authority and strategies of legitimisation of authority because ancient Indian political thinkers knew that the legitimate political authority was needed to secure regular obedience from the people. In the literature on political science, the word *Danda* was used to denote political authority and the science of politics was called *Dandaniti.* Essentially, there were three stages of development of the concept of political authority in ancient India. The first phase was Vedic phase in which religious sanctions and performance of sacrifices formed important means of constitution of political authority. During the second phase, when the states assumed territorial identity, the concept of social contract was used as an important instrument of formation of political authority. In the third phase, when there emerged big states with multi-ethnic populations the concept of divinity of the king was used even though this concept of divinity was rooted in contractual origin. During later two phases of development, religion continued to exercise influence on the process of formation of political authority.

Three Theories of Origin of Kingship in Vedic Literature

During the Vedic period, the kingdom was slowly assuming the territorial form and in the post-Vedic period, we could see the emergence of *Janapada* states. The *Janapada* states not only assumed territorial identity, but they also developed ideological position of their states (Agrawala, 1963: 473-80). But the impact of the Vedic ceremonies was there. It was through these ceremonies that the relationship with gods was established. The king's path of life was 'Karma-Marga' and as a result, he had to perform sacrifices. In the discussion, we shall first see how political authority in the Vedic India was constituted and subsequently, we shall discuss how this authority was legitimised through the consecration ceremony.

According to Dr. U. N. Ghoshal, there were three theories of origin of kingship in the Vedic literature and these theories were – the theory of divine creation, the theory of election of the king and the theory of social contract in its embryonic form.

The divine origin of kingship was the major concern of most of the Vedic literature. In the Vedic literature is included four *Vedas*, Vedic Samhitas including different *Brahmanas* and the *Aranyakas* and the *Upanishads*. The *Upanishads* are called the *Vedanta*. In the *Tattiriya Samhita*, the concept of divine creation of the kingship was expounded. It was said that the *Prajapati* created gods and demons. But he didn't create king. But gods prayed him to create Indra-king of gods. As a result, he created Indra and entered into his person. Under the leadership of Indra, gods defeated demons (Ghoshal, 1966: 27). Indra's leadership was accepted by gods when he acquired the luster of Prajapati. When Indra did not have the luster of Prajapati, gods did not accept him as their king. (28) In the *Jaiminiya Brahmana* it is said that Varuna wanted to become king. Hence, he requested *Prajapati* to confer kingship on him. Prajapati taught him a 'mantra'. After the recital of the 'Mantra', he was made to sit on the throne of the king and was consecrated. All gods accepted him as the king. Thus, Varuna owed his kingship to the divine blessings of Prajapati. (28)

First Theory

In the Vedic literature, especially in the *Rigveda* and the *Atharva Veda*, king's affinity to god was established. In the Rigveda (X. 173) the poet prayed gods for making king's rule stable and compel the subjects to pay their contribution to the king. In the following stanza, the poet prayed that the king might succeed in attaining sovereignty and he might be free from his rivals. (X 174) In these prayers, close relationship between gods and king was established. king was identified with king of gods that was Indra. It is pointed out by Dr. Coomarswami that according to ancient thinkers, kingship was not originated because of social contract nor was it elective in the sense that his actions represented will of the majority of the people or those of secular ministers but he was a ruler by the divine right. He was ordained to rule by the will of god. (Coomarswami, 1979: 16) Various sacrifices were performed to invest divine power in the person of the king.

Second Theory

Second theory of origin of kingship was that of election. In the *Rigveda* the king was elected by the people or by the Brahamanas, *Kshatriya* and the *Vaishyas*. It is said that for their own welfare and well-being, *Vish* or the people had elected the king (Kangle, 1969: 24). The kingship in the Vedic India was elective and he was elected through consensus. During the Vedic period, the people had a right to elect the king as well as they had a right to banish the king from his kingdom. The *Atharvaveda* called the banished king as 'aparuddha' and he had to win back the favour of the *Vish* to stage come back. (24-25)

The *Tattiriya Samhita* tells us that gods and demons were in conflict and gods suffered defeat because they did not have any leader. Therefore, they decided to elect Soma as their king. After his election, they conquered the demons. The *Aitereya Brahmana* informs us that at the time of great consecration ceremony it is declared that "he is of the gods the mightiest, the most powerful the strongest, the most real and the best, hence we consecrate him." (28) Then all gods accepted his leadership and bestowed the title of sovereignty on him. In the theory of election of kings, two principles were expounded. First, the king was elected to fight war against the enemy and secondly, he was elected by the gods because he was the most qualified to be the leader.

Third Theory

According to Dr. Ghoshal, there was the third theory of origin of kingship which had contractual roots. *Vishvarupa* in his commentary on the *Yajnya Valkya Smriti* makes mention of it on the authority of some lost *Brahmana* work. It informs us that gods and men (or sages) failed to bring men under their control through benevolence. As a result, gods disappeared. Prajapati asked gods who should protect the earth after their disappearance? The people devoid of protection would grow sinful and wouldn't give their offerings to gods on which their own livelihood depended. Gods then decided to create a king in human form after taking essential elements from all gods. He secured qualities of beauty, luster, prowess, renunciation and restraint. When the king insisted on securing the help of law or *dharma*, the same was created for protection. The coercive authority or *danda* is the cause of *dharma* and the king who knows this inflicts *danda* even on his erring father! This theory of origin of state is interesting as it puts forward four important propositions– (1) In the pre-political conditions, the people were ruled by gods and sages with the help of benevolence as there was no need of *danda*. (2) There was anarchy with the disappearance of gods as they couldn't rule with the help of benevolence. (3) Gods created king in the human form taking divine attributes from different gods to rule over the people. (4) The king sought to take help of the principle of *danda* and *dharma* to create discipline in the people. (Ghoshal, 29) It is rightly pointed out by Dr Ghoshal that this theory anticipated many of the arguments developed in the *Shantiparva*.

In the *Rigveda*, the divine nature and divine creation of kingship was constantly emphasised. Divine favours were invoked. (10.173-74) The king prayed that he should secure kingdom as well as victory with the help of gods. (10-174. 3-4)

Vedic Sacrifices

In the Vedic literature, the divine nature of kingship was emphasised and it is argued that it is ultimately related to performance of sacrifices. In this endeavour, the king was helped by *Purohits* because through the good offices of Purohit only, divinity was bestowed on the king. In the *Purush Sukta*, of the *Rigveda*, the divine sacrifice of divine cosmic Man was described. This primeval cosmic sacrifice was performed to ensure proper organisation of world and human society. (De Bary, 1969: 17) The purpose of sacrifice was to secure *rashtra* or kingdom and *Kshatra* or political power to the king. According to the *Aitereya Brahmana,* if the *Purohita* was appeased, he carried kingdom to heavenly world. He could secure kingdom, political power and the people. (Pandey, 1978: 75) Thus, the kingship was identified with kingdom and the people or *Vish*. The *Atharvaveda* tells us that *rashtra* is *Kshatra* which means kingdom is political power. (77) Along with, *Rashtra* and *Kshatra, Swaraj* was the third concept used by ancient Vedic thinkers. Its meaning is variously given. One meaning of Swaraj was self-government.

Brahma and Kshatra

The *Kshatra* or ruling power was closely related to *Rajanya* or ruling class. There was third element which was called *Vish* or the Vaishyas and the Shudras. The *Vish* was dependent on the king. According to the *Shatapatha Brahmana*, by performing certain sacrifices, the Kshatriya became the ruler of the people and by another rite the priest made *Vish* obedient to the king. (90) But both were interdependent. Hence, Dr. Pandey writes, "*Kshatra* is politically superior to the *Vish* but at the same time, the *Vish* was the source and vigour of the *Kshatra* because the latter was supported by *Vish*." (91)

But for that purpose, the king had to perform a number of sacrifices. In the Vedic literature, the king is asked to perform three different sacrifices – the three sacrifices are – the Vajapeya sacrifice, the *Rajasuya* sacrifice and the Ashvamedha sacrifice. Performance of these sacrifices is necessary and the priests played an important role in it. According to Dr. Coomarswami, the consecration ceremony, which was a part of these sacrifices was a marriage formula and in this formula, there is a marriage between *Brahma* and *Kshatra* which represent masculine and femine elements. *Brahma* is represented by the priest and *Kshatra* is represented by the king. Also, it is a marriage between the sky and the earth. (Commarswami, 34-36)

The Vajapeya Sacrifice

The first sacrifice was Vajapeya sacrifice which was the sacrifice of drinks and races. The king and the sacrifice's chariot was declared victorious. After the race, 17 drums were beaten. Then king was consecrated, as water was besprinkled on his throne. After the performance of the sacrifice, the priest said that the gods should quicken him that nobody should be his rival for dominant political power and supremacy. His rule is established over the people and kingdom (Janrajya). With the declaration on the priest, "This son of a father, mother and a tribe is your king. Soma is the king of Brahmins." (Pandey, 51)

The Rajasuya Sacrifice

The second important sacrifice was the *Rajasuya* sacrifice in which the king was consecrated. The preliminary ceremony of the sacrifice started with initiation on the first day. On the first day of the month of Falguna which was followed by offerings to *Anumati* and *nirrti*. The next programme was *Ratnavamshi* ceremony in which *Ratnins* or *Rajkartarhas* or king makers as well as wives of the king took part. On the first day of month of Chaitra, he was anointed and water brought from different rivers, oceans, lakes and holy places was besprinkled on his head. He wore new dress and shot three arrows. He was again consecrated by a Brahmin, a Rajanya and a Vaishya representing all classes of society. Then the king went out in a chariot to fight a mock battle and won cows in it. The 'looted' property was distributed among the priests and Rajanyas. Then he sat on the throne which was placed on tiger skin. He took five dices from the officiating priest. He was gently beaten on the back by the priest with a sacred stick. After that a wooden sword was given to him. The dice was played and the king was declared victor. After that the king took bath and made sacrificial offerings to Indra and Vishnu. (Pandey, 54-56) After the performance of these ceremonies, the priest likened the sacrificer to different gods. He declared that the king had become the lord of *Samrajya*. (57-58) Before the performance of *Aindrabhisheka*, the *ratnins* declared that "Oh! People, a lord of world has taken birth. He is eater of the people. He is a destroyer of enemies, protector of Brahmins and guardian of *Dharma*."

The Horse Sacrifice

The last sacrifice was horse sacrifice which was performed by the kings to establish their royal authority. Only the king was eligible to perform this sacrifice. It was performed to secure alround prosperity to the kingdom. In this sacrifice, the sacrificial horse was set free to wander in the different directions for a year. It was protected by hundreds of soldiers. During that period, the officiating priest narrated the stories of past history and that of great kings. The horse returned back after a year. Then in the ceremony it was sacrificed. (71)

The horse sacrifice was a war model for rulers to conquer territories of their enemies as it involved establishment of his sovereignty over other kingdoms. The *Brihadaranyaka Upanishada* (1.1.1) added cosmic dimension to it by comparing various parts of horse with different organs of the universe. It is dedication of different organs of the universe in the cause of general welfare.

Constitutional Significance

In the *Rajasuya* ceremony following *Ratnins* played an important role-

1. Purohita -Royal chaplain
2. Senapati -Chief of the army
3. Gramani -Village headman
4. Suta -Charioteer
5. Kshatta -Chief of servants
6. Bhagadugha -Distributor of wealth
7. Govikarta -Arranger of food
8. Akshavapa -Officer of dice playing
9. Taksha -Carpenter
10. Palagala -Messenger
11. Sangrahita -One who declares royal orders
12. Rathakara -Maker of chariots

Apart from these 12 *ratnins*, three queens of the king also took part in it. They were *Mahishi* or the queen, *Parivrikta* (abandoned queen) Vavata the queen liked by the king. Thus, there were 15 ratnins who took part in the ceremony. (Kangle, 1969: 29-30) In the *Rajasuya*, these people offered kingship to the king by handing over *danda* to him. Each one personally handed it over. (26-27)

Dr. Ghoshal has elaborately discussed the significance of these sacrifices. According to him, the *Rajasuya* conferred kingship and sovereignty to the king. Secondly, when the priest had gently beaten the king on the back, he thereby declared that he was 'adandya' or above law. According to the *Shatapatha Brahmana*, he was exempted from *danda* as he was above it. Thirdly, the sacrificer attained the divine attributes because of performance of these sacrifices. (Ghoshal, 24-25) Ghoshal was of the view that the king derived his authority including immunity from punishment because of performance of the sacrifices. (25) There is a mention of fourth sacrifice which is called *Sautramani* sacrifice. It was a part of *Rajasuya* sacrifice and by performance of this sacrifice, the *Kshatriya* was assured of his victory and the king who was dethroned from the power was restored to his kingdom. (Pandey, 63) The name of this sacrifice was derived from Sutramana who was called protector or good deliverer. Ensuring personal well-being was the motive behind performance of this sacrifice. (63-65)

Dharma and Legitimacy

The royal authority of the king was legitimised with the help of performance of different sacrifices. The performance was closely related to the concept of *dharma* and it is argued that the concept of *dharma* was based on truth. According to the *Shatapatha Brahmana*, due to performance of *Rajasuya* sacrifice, Varuna, made the sacrificer *dharmapati* or a lord of *dharma*. Quoting a formula of another *Rajasuya* ritual, the same work boldly transferred the epithet *dharmavritta* or upholder of *dharma* in the original from god Varuna to the human king. In the *Aitereya Brahmana*, after the performance of 'Aindrabhisheka' the king was declared as '*dharmasya gopta*' or protector of *dharma*. (Ghoshal, 23)

The law of *dharma* is based on truth or *rita* as it regulates internal relationship between man and man, man and other classes in the society and man and the state. In the *Rigveda*, the *Purush-sukta* talked about four classes of the society as parts or four organs of the cosmic man. Brahmins, Kshatriyas, Vaishyas and Shudras formed four classes of the society. But some later *Brahmana Samhitas* denied divine status to the Shudras as they started saying that Shudra was untruth and they sprang from evil, hence, they could not be the part of divine scheme. (Ghoshal, 31) Thus, there were two schools in the Vedic thought as one included Shudra in the divine scheme and other sought to exclude him! Hence, how to establish co-relationship between truth and social discrimination was the major problem before Indian social thinkers.

In the Vedic society- the four classes were divided into two- Brahmins and Kshatriyas formed ruling class and the numerous class of Vaishyas and Shudras formed *Vish* or people. Though the Brahmins, because of their control over the ritual practices claimed that they were superior to the class of rajanyas, but in the *Rajasuya* ritual, it was made clear that *Brahma* was *inferior* to *Kshatra* as it had to obey the orders of the king. In the *Taittiriya Samhita*, it is made clear that all three varnas – Brahmins, Vaishyas and Shudras have to obey the orders of the king. (33) The class of *Vish* was important because it supported the kingdom.

There is further development of the idea of *dharma* as political power in the Upanishadic period. In a celebrated passage in the *Brihadaranyaka Upanishada* there is a description of divine creation of social order. The *Upanishad* (1.4, 11-14) said that initially the *Brahma* existed alone but since he was alone, he could not perform duties of the world. Hence, he created *Kshatra* and there was no greater authority than Kshatriya, hence, in the *Rajasuya* sacrifice, Brahmin had to sit below Kshatriya. But after creating a class of Kshatriyas also, *Brahma* could not complete his duties, hence, he created a class of Vaishyas. But with the help of class of Vaishyas also, he couldn't completely perform his daily functions, hence the class of Shudras was created. The Shudras sustained the world. But after the creation of four classes also, *Brahma* couldn't perform his ordained functions. Hence, he created the principle of *dharma* which could control Kshatriyas also. It is king of kings and with the help of this principle even the weak could rule over the strong. *Dharma* is based on truth, therefore, it is said that those who speak truth speak *dharma*. Both *dharma* and truth are inseparable".

This passage in the *Upanishada* made it clear that *dharma* was the king of kings and as a ruling principle, it exercised control over all classes of the society. This passage establishes four important principles–

(1) Originally, social order is divine creation but in reality, four classes in the society were created to fulfill growing material needs of the society- as the functional specialisation required creation of new classes.

(2) Even after creation of four classes, *Brahma* could not perform his ordained functions, hence the concept of *dharma* was created to regulate the relationship.

(3) The principle of *dharma* was the king of kings and therefore, a weak person could rule over the strong with the help of *dharma*. Here, *dharma* implied laws of state which enabled the weak person to rule over the strong.

(4) *Dharma* is based on truth and truth is legitimising principle of *dharma*.

Thus, in this passage, the *Brihadaranyaka Upanishada* firmly established *dharma* as the basis of political authority. It regulated relationship between different classes as well as between the classes and the state.

The Concept of Danda

The concept of *danda* is used to denote political authority. *Danda* or rod symbolises the power of the state. Therefore, the most ancient name for political science is *Dandaniti* or the science of punishment. Kautilya said that the proper use of *danda* was necessary. When it was used justly, it endowed subjects with *dharma*, *artha* and *kama*. Used unjustly, whether in passion, anger or in contempt, it enraged even forest anchorites and wandering ascetics, how more than to the householders? If not used at all, it gave rise to the logic of fishes, for, the stronger swallowed the weaker in the absence of weilder of *danda*; protected by him, it prevailed. (14.3-15) Thus, it was the argument of Kautilya that the proper use of *danda* was necessary for enjoyment of *dharma*, *artha* and *kama*.

Considering the importance of *danda*, Bhishma in the *Shantiparva* pointed out that *Danda* was important because *dharma* was dependent on *Danda*. In the *Shantiparva*, Arjuna advocated the cause of *Danda* and said that because of *Danda* only, *Yoga-Kshema* of the people was maintained. He pointed out that there were three important causes that forced people to obey the order of the king. They were as follows :

(1) Fear of punishment of the king.

(2) Fear of reprisals and retaliation from fellow human beings.

(3) Fear of punishment by the Lord of Death Yama in the next world.

It is the contention of Arjuna that the people sleep peacefully at night because *Danda* guarded them. It punished the wrong doer. (12.15-18) He said that fear was one of the elements that conditioned the behaviour of the men in society. (Bhattacharya, 2002: 98)

In the *Shantiparva*, Bhishma made a long argument in favour of *Danda*. While explaining the nature of *Danda*, Bhishma said that *danda* was dependent in *Dharma* and while applying *Danda*, the principle of *Dharma* had to be kept in mind. Proper application of *Danda* ensured proper promotion of three *Purusharthas*. *Danda* had a divine character as all gods resided in *Danda*. (12.121. 10-11) He pointed out that *Danda* was respected by the *acharyas* of different schools of thought. *Danda* assumed different forms such as avoiding harsh words, payment of gold, torture, banishment or execution but it had to be used by following the principles of justice. In conclusion, he pointed out that *Danda* remained awakened when the people took rest. (12-121)

Thus, ancient Indian thinkers closely identified *Danda* with *Dharma* and viewed the former as the symbol of political authority.

Constitution of Political Authority- theories of origin of kingship

In ancient societies, constitution of political authority was connected with the origin of kingship and in ancient India, three different theories of origin of kingship were expounded. The theories of origin of state threw light on the legitimisation of political authority. Following were three theories of origin of state –

(1) Theory of election of king,

(2) Theory of divine origin of king,

(3) Theory of social contract.

Election of the King

As far as the Vedic literature is concerned, we have several examples of election of king by the *Vish*. Professor Kangle pointed out that during the Vedic period, the people or *Vish* had a right to elect king as well as they had a right to banish the king from his kingdom. (Kangle, 24-25) We have discussed this earlier.

Election of the king was a recurring theme in ancient Indian political thought. In the *Jatakas*, there are at least two stories that described the election of the king. In the Uluka *Jataka* (No. 270) it is said that the birds had come together to elect the king as they realised that only birds didn't have the king. They elected crane as the Chairman of their general assembly. He invited nominations. Only Owl's name was proposed and seconded. The president asked birds three times whether they accepted the proposal. But at the third call, the crow came rushing and opposed the nomination. The crow said that when it was in jubilant mood, the owl was looking fearsome, how much more fearsome he would look if he got enraged! There was disorder. Birds accepted the objections of the crow and in its place, golden crane was elected as the king. In the Nachcha *Jataka* (32) there is an account of election of the king by men, animals, birds as fishes elected monster fish as the king after the example of animals. (Ghoshal, 66-67)

In the *Jataka* stories, there is a mention of election of Bodhisattva as king by the citizens when there was no king. In the *Katha Sarit Sagar* and the *Rajatarangini* also, there was mention of election of kings. (Please see Chapter V for details)

Second theory of origin of state was that of divine origin and we earlier had discussed how the king was divinely created. In the Mahabharata, it was said that the first king Manu was sent by Lord Brahma. Therefore, in the Mahabharata, the Quasi-divine, quasi-contractual theory of origin of state was expounded.

Theory of Social Contract of Origin of Kingship

Social contract theory of origin of king ship was an ancient theory of origin of kingship and in the Republic of Plato, there was a mention of this theory. (The Republic, 358b – 359c). In ancient India, all three traditions- Vedic, Buddhist and the *Smriti* or *Dharmashastra,* supported theory of social contract.

Vedic Roots of Social Contract

According to Professor Ghoshal, one could see the roots of social contract theory in the Vedic literature. In the *Aitereya Brahmana*, at the time of 'Aindrabhisheka' it is said, "The gods with Prajapati said, he is of the gods the mightiest, the most powerful, the strongest, the most real. The best to accomplish. Let us consecrate him, be it, they said and consecrated Indra." (28)

Dr. Ghoshal pointed out that in the Vedic literature, there was a mention of voluntary agreement of members of the community of gods to consolidate the authority of political society. Among the ceremonies of Soma sacrifice, there is a ceremony of Tanunapat which means a covenant made by the sacrificer and the priests in the name of god Tanunapat by which they pledge themselves not to injure each other. (29) The *Tattiriya Samhita* tells us that the gods and demons were in conflict and gods failed because they didn't have any leader. They got scattered in four directions. They reflected and decided to deposit their bodies in the house of Varuna and declared that those who transgressed the rules would cause trouble. They deposited their bodies in the house of Varuna, therefore, it could be called bodily covenant or *Tanunapatra*. This covenant was supported by solemn sanctions for the surrender of their distinct personalities in favour of divine ruler. (30) This covenant didn't create new political authority but it had consolidated pre-existing divine political authority.

In the *dharmasutra* literature, there is no mention of social contract but three themes that continuously dominate the discussion in the *Smriti*-literature find place there. The themes are- first, it is the duty of the king to protect citizens and their property. The king is liable to restore stolen property of its owners or he should pay its value to the owner out of his own treasury. (50)

Secondly, the people should pay one-sixth of the produce of land to the king in the form of taxes. This is a fee the king charges for the protection he extends.

Thirdly, ultimately, proper performance of his duties is divinely ordained function of the Kshatriyas. Thus, proper discharge of duties is an important function of the king. (50)

Social contract theory of origin of state is based on three important principles –

(1) Prevalence of state of nature and need of the establishment of state,

(2) The contract between the concerned parties for creation of political authority,

(3) Terms of political contract and the obligation of citizens.

Buddhist Theory of Origin of Kingship

In the 'Digha Nikaya' Buddha expounded his theory of origin of kingship under the section the 'book of genesis'. In the process, he expounded the theory of origin of Kshatriya mandala by criticising the Vedic dogma of divine creation of social order. One of the important aspects of Buddha's theory of origin of state was that he didn't conceive divine intervention.

In his discussion on origin of state, Buddha first discussed creation and dissolution of the world. In the initial stage of development, human beings didn't have material bodies and they could traverse easily in air or in water. They were self-luminous. But the earth got distinguished from water, sun, moon and the stars and the constellations became visible, the seasons, months and years made their appearance. They being continued lived off the earth. As the greed entered the heart, the beings lost their etheral existence and acquired material form. The vegetation appeared on the earth first of low order and subsequently of high order. The husk free self-ripening rice appeared and the beings got themselves fed upon it. They acquired more solidity of their bodies. Differences of self emerged with resulting passions among men and women. Subsequently, men and women developed lust and greed in their minds and decided to build their own households and began to store rice in their houses. As soon as men started doing this, the self-ripening rice disappeared. But they learnt to cultivate land and produced rice. In the course, they distributed and divided land among themselves. Certain greedy person, guarding his own plot stole the rice of other person. As a result, others arrested and censured him, for this act of theft. They made him promise not to do this again. But he or someone else continued to steal others' property. There was physical violence and quarrels. Thus, there appeared four evils of theft, censure, lying and violence. To overcome this, men gathered together, lamented appearance of these evils and decided to create an authority which would put stop to this. They decided to elect a person as their chief, who was the most handsome and capable. He should punish the person who had committed guilt, and he should censure the person who deserved to be censured and should banish the one who deserved banishment. He should perform his duties in the spirit of righteousness. In return of that, the people promised the chosen person that they would pay him one-sixth of portion of rice that they produced. They elected the most handsome and the most capable person as the ruler. He was called 'Mahasammata' or great elect. He was also called Kshatriya or the lord of fields, who guarded them. He was also called Raja because he gratified others. (Ghoshal, 63-64)

The election of the *Mahasammata* set the process of beginning of division of the society in different classes. The election signified the emergence of class of Kshatriyas. Those who lived in forest, studied Vedas and mediated were called Brahmanas. Brahmana means one who puts evil away. Those who were proficient in trade were called Vaishyas and those who were skillful in hunting and different crafts were called Shudras. Buddha concluded his narrative saying, "their origin was from those beings and no others. Unto themselves and not unlike and it took place according to *Dharma* and not according to its reverse." (65)

This account of the origin of kingship was not based on actual history but it was based on a peculiar logic developed by Lord Buddha. There are three salient features of this theory of origin of kingship. Firstly, kingship was not divinely created but emerged out of social contract. Secondly, public authority was created to establish an order in the society when there was division of property in the society. The basic principle of social contract was the protection offered by the king and the taxes paid by the people to him in lieu of protection. Thirdly, creation of the state was a gradual development as at first the institutions of family, private property and class were created. The contract was bi-lateral in character.

Kautilya on Social Contract Theory of Origin of Kingship

The *arthashastra- Smriti* tradition developed the theory of social contract which was influenced by Buddhist theory as well as by the proto-theories of social contract expounded in the Vedic literature. In the *arthashastra* of Kautilya there is a mention of the theory in the chapter "Keeping watch on seducible and non-seducible parties in one's own country." He said that the secret agents of the king opposing another should carry on disputations at holy places, assemblies, communal gatherings and the congregations of the people about the authority of the king. One of them should say, "this king is said to be endowed with all virtues and yet no virtue is to be seen in him, as he oppresses citizens and country people with taxes and fines". The others should contradict him saying "the people overwhelmed by the law of fishes, made Manu, the son of Vivasvata their king and they assigned one-sixth of the grains, one-tenth of the commodities and money as his share." Maintained by that, kings bring about the well-being and security of the subjects. Those who do not pay taxes and fines take in themselves the sins of those kings who do not bring about well-being and security of the people. Therefore, even forest dwellers offer sixth part of their gleaned grains saying, "this is the share for him who protects us. This is the office of Indra and Yama. King's wrath and favour is visibly manifest. Even divine punishments strike those who slight them. Therefore, the kings must not be slighted." (Arth. 1.13- 2.12)

This theory is expounded in the backdrop of security of the state. Therefore, spies are asked to ascertain contentedness or otherwise of the people who live on his grain, cattle and money who help them at the time of calamities or prosperity who restrain rebellious kinsmen or region in these who repell attack of an enemy or a rebel forest chieftain. (1.13.1-5) Kautilya expounds the theory through the mouth of spies with the specific purpose of legitimising authority of the king and to secure continuous obedience of his subjects. He makes it clear that due to existence of king only, the condition of 'matsya Nyaya' or the logic of fishes was prevented. The people made Manu king and promised him that in return of protection, they would pay him taxes and if the people did not pay taxes to the king, they would invite the sins committed by the kings. King was divinely created and divine punishments visited those who showed disrespect to the king. (Kangle, 1969: 16)

Theory of social contract of origin of kingship was essentially a myth of legitimisation and the fact became clear in different theories of origin of the state in the Mahabharata. In the *Shantiparva* of the great epic, we could see mature synthesis of *arthashastra* and the *Smriti* traditions.

Theories of Origin of Kingship in the Mahabharata

There are three theories of origin of kingship in the *Shantiparva*. All these theories throw light on constitution of political authority. One could discern three strands in theories of social contract. Firstly, the state was created to overcome the logic of fishes. Secondly, the state was created out of social contract between the king and the people in which the latter agreed to pay taxes in return of protection promised to them. Thirdly, along with social contract, divine intervention is also sought to legitimise the authority of the king because Manu- the first king was sent by god Brahma.

In the Chapter 59 of the *Shantiparva*, Yudhishthira asked Bhishma to explain why the king possessed the specific power to punish or reward the people, when, in fact he was an ordinary human being like other human beings. (12.59, 10-12) Bhishma told him that the kingship grew with the changes in the epoch. In the first age of truth, there was no king and there was no kingship, there was no punishment and no punisher. The people protected each other by following the principles of *Dharma*. But slowly there was decline of moral standards among the people. They were influenced by avarice and greed. They were moved by anger and lost sense of discrimination. They got scared of anarchy and lawlessness and requested Lord *Brahma* to interfere. He decided to interfere. He thought that instead of creating king, it would be better if a book on science of politics is drafted first. Hence, the lord prepared a book on *Dandaniti* or politics. It is interesting to note that the great epic pointed out that before the origin of state, there was a need of preparation of book on politics. There is a clear description of content of this book on Politics which was huge in size. Politics is governed by *danda*, therefore, this book was called *Dandaniti*. This divine book on *Dandaniti* was abridged by different gods, and sages.

The people went to Lord Vishnu to request him to designate a king for them. Vishnu created a son called Virajas from his own body who was luminous like sun. But Viraj had no desire to rule as he preferred life of renunciation. He was followed by kings like Kirtiman, Kardam and Ananga. Ananga's son Atibal became slave of passions. He married Sunitha. They begot a son called Vena who, after assuming the royalty, did not behave properly with the people. As a result, the people were not happy. Hence, he was killed by the sages with the help of *mantras* and they procreated a young man called Prithu out of Vena's body. He was called Adiraj. They begot a son out of right thigh of the dead king who was called *Nishad*. The tribal population of *Nishads* and the *Pulindas* belong to him. They inhabited in the jungles and mountains.

Prithu was trained in the Vedas and the Science of Politics. Hence, he asked the sages, "I have possessed a fine understanding of nature of *dharma* and *artha* in what way should I use my knowledge?" The sages advised him to pursue the path of *dharma*, imbibe the principle of equanimity, abandon six enemies of senses, and punish those who do not follow the principles of *dharma*. They further told him that he should protect Brahmins. He should follow the principles enshrined in the science of politics and shouldn't behave capriciously. (12-59)

Prithu accepted the advise of the sages and told them that he would respect Brahmins and govern the state according to the principles of politics. He established order in the society. He entertained the people, hence, he was called Raja and he protected Brahmins from the wounds, hence he was called Kshatriya! Since he was chosen by god Vishnu therefore, he should be considered as god in human form. Nobody should disobey the order of the king because gods had established him on the throne; therefore, the people believed that god and king were equal in standing.

If we carefully scrutinise this account of origin of kingship, we could see that the king originated first due to intervention of the gods. Prithu owed his origin to his father Vena as well as sages. The king owed his kingship to the sages who installed him on the throne. He appointed many of them as his ministers and promised them that he would rule the earth with the help of the book on politics and protect the people as if they were gods. (12.59-112) There was no contract with the people, therefore, there was no mention of relations between taxation and protection.

Dread of Anarchy

In the Mahabharata, Bhishma has expounded a social contract theory which is the expansion of the theory expounded in the *arthashastra* of Kautilya. This theory was expounded in the background of dread of anarchy. It was the argument of the epic that in the anarchy, life of man became precarious as property and wealth of the people was looted by thieves. The people couldn't pursue trade, agriculture and cattle breeding and as a result, they would not get sources of livelihood. They wouldn't be in a position to organise any social function out of fear of disruption. Hence, the king should protect kingdom to overcome anarchy. The king should imbibe the principles of 'Vinaya' (education in principles of politics) and learn how to govern the state according to principles of 'anushasana'. 'Anushasana' means governance of the country according to the principles of righteousness. (12-68)

Social Contract Theory in the Mahabharata

Yudhishthira has asked Bhishma to tell him the duties of kingdom. Yudhishthira told him that it was the duty of the kingdom to consecrate some one as the king because without king, kingdom became very weak. In the state where anarchy prevailed, the weak people were destroyed by the strong. The logic of fishes prevailed. No one should live in the kingdom which was torn by anarchy. Those who lived in country where anarchy prevailed they couldn't enjoy their life. During times of anarchy, the sinful man enjoyed by robbing other's wealth, but, when, however, his ill-acquired wealth was taken away by others, he wished for the king. The wealth of one was taken away by two and wealth of two was taken away by many. It was clear that in times of anarchy, even the wicked persons could not be happy. Bhishma then talked about the original contract between the men. According to this contract, they agreed upon following principles –

(1) One who becomes harsh in speech and violent in temper, he, who seduced others' wives or robbed others' property, would be renounced by all.

(2) Enact uniform rules for all classes in order to create confidence in the minds of the people.

The people lived peacefully for some time adhering to this contract. But they couldn't live peacefully any more as there was no one to enforce the rules. Therefore, the people went to Brahma and said that due to non-existence of the king, their life had become miserable. They said, "Please give us king who would be worthy of respect and capable of our protection." (12-67) Brahma asked Manu to accept the kingship but he was not willing to assume kingship.

Brahma asked him about the cause of his reluctance. He said, "I do not want to perform cruel deeds which kingship entailed me to perform. It was difficult to rule over men who followed the path of untruth."

The people promised Manu that he shouldn't fear because the sins committed by men would affect those who committed it. They said, 'For increase of your wealth, we shall give you 50th part of our gold, and animals and 10th part of our grain. All brave and leading men of the society would follow you. You protect us and fourth part of our merit will belong to you." (12.67) Manu accepted this offer. After seeing his prowess, the people started following their duties and the order was established in the world. Hence, men should elect and crown a king, bedecked with all his emblems and respect him.

In this theory of social contract, constitution of political authority was visualised out of social contract in order to overcome state of nature. In this theory the king was not chosen by the people but he was sent by the god. Thus, in this theory also there is divine element involved. But still, there is a contract or 'Samaya' between the king and the people in the sense that the king promised to protect the people and the people in turn promised to pay taxes to him.

Social Contract Theory of Kapavya

There is the third theory of social contract in the Mahabharata. This is a very interesting theory in the sense that it tells how the kingship emerged in the tribal communities. In the jungle, there used to live a Dasyu called Kapavya who was a man of great qualities. He used to serve his parents as well as he helped the sages living in the jungle. He had developed good knowledge of time and place and he followed the principles of righteousness.

One day hundreds of the tribals living in the villages gathered together and requested Kapavya to become their chief. They said, "You are brave and knowledgeable person and you have knowledge of time and place, hence, we request you to assume our leadership and protect us." (12-133) He said that he would accept their request provided that they agreed to follow the rules laid down by him. The rules were as follows :

(1) They should not kill women, children, ascetics and those people who did not want to fight war.

(2) They should protect cows and Brahmins.

(3) They should not disrupt marriages or other ceremonies organised by the people.

(4) They shouldn't destroy standing crops and fruit bearing trees.

(5) *Danda* is created not to kill the people but to protect them and they should punish those who gathered wealth by plundering his own country. Bhishma said that those Dasyus agreed and followed the principles of the *Dharmashastra* earned great merit. (12-133)

This is a very interesting story in the sense that it shows how ancient Indian social thinkers tried to incorporate tribal elements in the Indian society. They gave internal autonomy and choice of selection of leadership to the people but at the same time, they sought to incorporate the *Dharmashastra*'s principles of government in the performance of duties. It is the opinion of Dr. V. S. Agrawala that the episode must be based on the life of some tribal king and this must have been incorporated in the great epic during the Gupta period. (Agrawala, 1968: III 113-14) In this social contract, the king laid down certain conditions and the people agreed to follow them. The people had desired to overcome state of nature.

Thus, in different theories of origin of kingship in ancient India, there is discussion on how political authority was constituted and why was it essential on the part of the people to obey the same. The theories of social contract were essentially the theories of legitimisation of political authority.

Strategies of Legitimisation of Authority

Ancient Indian political thinkers understood the importance of legitimisation of political authority because they knew that without legitimate political authority, the people would not willingly obey the orders of the king. The main concern of any political authority was how to obtain regular obedience from the people. In ancient India, three methods were suggested to legitimise authority of the king. They werc as follows:

(1) The authority of the king is legitimised by organising consecration ceremony. It was a religious ceremony which gave divine sanction to the king to rule. The royal chaplain officiated this ceremony. This was the most popular method of legitimisation of authority in all ancient and medieval societies.

(2) It was pointed out that his orders should be obeyed not because he was god in human form but because he upheld the cause of dharma and protected lives and properties of the people.

(3) The authority of the king should be obeyed because it was based on righteousness. The king acquired moral authority when he followed the principles of *dharma*. The righteous king won respect of the people. Hence, the Mahabharata said: "One who is respected by his own people, becomes an object of esteem with enemies also, while one who is disregarded by his own people is set at naught by his enemies." (12.69.34)

There is a close relationship between righteousness and divinity of king as the Indian theory was different from that of the Western theory of divine rights. In the Western theory, the king was divinely ordained to rule, therefore, he could do no wrong. But in India, the king's divine nature was ultimately based on his virtuous behaviour because the king who ceased to be a righteous, did not qualify to be the divine king. It was pointed out that his orders should be obeyed not because he was god in human form because he upheld the cause of *dharma* and protected lives and properties of the people. Due to this only, the ruler was called *'rashtrabhrita'* or the sustainer of the country. (Chousalkar, 1976: 58-70) In the Mahabharata, Bhishma told the king that he should recognise the fact that his authority was always limited.

Dr Coomarswami on Authority

It is the opinion of Dr. Anand Coomarswami that the Indian concept of authority was complex in nature as it continuously mediated between the spiritual authority and the temporal power. Though the temporal power had to constantly use *danda* to punish the wrong doer, it was always desired that it should be sparingly used. It was his contention that the sacrifice of consecration was a marriage formula between the earth and the sky and *Brahma* (male) and *Kshatra* (female) which ensured that it would avert occurrence of death and famines in the kingdom. The king was directly responsible for the fertility of land as the fall of rain in season depended on his righteousness or default. (Coomarswami, 65) The temporal power sought to pursue its own independent path, hence, it had to be continuously controlled by the spiritual authority. According to him, in a traditional society, the oppressor was excommunicated or legally deposed, and it was followed by appointment of more regular successors in whom the kingship was reborn. In the anti-traditional societies, when the oppressor had been removed by the popular revolution, those who had been oppressed proposed to govern in their own interest and became the oppressors in turn. The majority oppressed the minority. This was followed by plutocracy or tyranny of one person whose rule was unprincipled. This caricature of monarchy prepared the way for the state of disorder which was called 'anrita'. (70-71)

According to Dr Coomarswami, in order to maintain internal economy of the state, the disorder had to be controlled by order, because man himself was city of god. The man had two selves- one outer and active and other inner and contemplative. The problem of internal economy by which the men's end could be attained in one of the relationships of psycho-physical ego to the spiritual person. (71) The king had to combine this outer and internal worlds of his soul because he had to control and conquer his senses. He had to enjoy autonomy and autonomy meant not to be ruled by the multitude, not to be ruled by one's own family and not to be ruled by one's own desires. (73) It was his contention that the king should become his own master by conquering his passions. Man's self had no other foe than the self. That self was a friend of self that had conquered itself. Therefore, only royal road to power was to become one's own Master. According to customary Indian policy, the rebellious vessal wasn't exterminated, but after the defeat, he was restored to his kingship and empowered to govern as a new friend of the emperor. The state of anxiety was replaced by the state of peace. According to Indian sociological theory, any individual tyranny and self-importance had led to disintegration and finally death of body politic- collective or individual. But ultimately self-government (Swaraj) depended on self-control. (85)

In ancient India, the spiritual authority legitimised the temporal power in order to establish people's faith in the efficacy of the government. Spiritual authority had a power to control temporal power but it could not replace the latter because the moment it tried to usurp power for itself, it had acted against the principles of *dharma* and as a result, it would lose its authority. Temporal power had to act according to principles of *dharma*, otherwise, it would also lose its sanction to govern.

The sages and Brahmins were instrumental in bringing about change in the government, but they did not assume the charge. They appointed a new king from the family of the deposed king or made the elephant choose the king from amongst citizens for, they knew that the spiritual authority had a limited role as far as the temporal affairs of the governance of state was concerned.

Political authority had to contend with the problem of erosion of its legitimacy and when erosion took place the people refused to obey the orders of the authority. King has to use force to secure compliance of his orders. If king was not in a position to achieve reconciliation with the people, the latter took recourse to protest. The protest began with the citizens lodging complaint to the king and it culminated in the armed uprising and rebellion of the people. Kautilya pointed out that change in ones own people-'Svajan Vikar' leads to uprising of the people. In the subsequent chapters we shall discuss the forms of protest devised by the Indian people to fight against the despots.

References

Agrawala, V. S. (1968), *Bharat-Savitri- I, II, III,* Sasta Sahitya, New Delhi.

Bary, D. C (Ed.) (1973), *Sources of Indian Tradition*, Motilal Banarasidas, Delhi.

Bhattacharya, S. C. (2002), *Secular and Pluralistic Elements in the Idea of State in Early India*, Indian Institute of Advanced Studies, Shimla.

Chousalkar, A. (1976), *Power, Authority and Legitimacy in Ancient India*, pp. 58-70, Political Science Review, Vol. 17.

Coomar, swami, A. (1979), *Spiritual Authority and Temporal Power in the Indian Theory of Government*, Munshiram Manoharlal, Delhi.

Ghoshal, U. N. (1966), *A History of Indian Political Ideas*, Oxford University Press, Mumbai.

Kangle, R. P. (1969), *Prachin Bharatiya Rajniti*, Mauj, Mumbai.

__________ (1966), *The Kautilya Arthashastra*, Part III, University of Mumbai, Mumbai.

Pandey, U. C. (1979), *Political Concepts and Institutions in the Shukla Yajurveda*, Janaki, Patna.

Chapter – III

Nature of State and Ideologies of Dissent in Early India

In our last chapter, we have seen how political authority was constituted in ancient India and what were the means used by ancient thinkers to legitimise it. In this chapter, we shall study the nature of state in ancient India, different ideologies of dissent and protest and analyse forms of political protest.

Changing Nature of State in Ancient India

As we have seen in our last chapter, the state in ancient India assumed the territorial form during the post-Vedic period when a large number of *Janapada* states were established. *Janapada*, during the post-Vedic period, was a political term as it referred to a small territorial state which had population of few lakh people, consisting of different classes and castes. (Kangle, R.P., 1969: 36) Different clans and tribes came together and got settled down in a particular area. Ruling class of the *Janapada* belonged to a dominant clan or *gana* of the state which took lead in the establishment of this settlement. The name of *Janapada* was styled after that clan only. In the process of development, it evolved political identity of its own. During the Buddhist period, we could see prevalence of high level of political consciousness in the *Janapada* states, therefore, it was favourably compared with the Greek city- states of that period (Agrawala, 1963: 469-93) This type of state flourished during the eighth century B.C.

to fourth century B.C. But the Nandas and the later on the Mauryas destroyed and incorporated them in their empire. Most of the ruling classes of these states belonged to *Kshatriya Varna*. Maha Padma Nanda destroyed them and claimed that he was second Parashurama.

The population of the *Janapada* was heterogeneous as with the development of agriculture, different classes of the society got settled in a particular territory. It is rightly pointed out by Dr. Mishra that "the term *Janapada* as such is a settlement on the territory occupied by *Jana* and marks that stage of evolution of the Vedic Indians when they became territorially conscious and founded the first series known as *Janapada* states." (Mishra, 1973: 8)

The *Janapada* state of mid fifth century was a subject of political analysis of the *arthashastra* tradition as it carried out an inductive investigation in the phenomenon of the state. The state that figured in the *Jataka* stories was essentially a *Janapada* state. But at the same time, the *Janapada* was trying to expand its boundaries. The state at that time consisted of two regions - *Pura* and *Janapada*. *Pura* stood for capital city and the *Janapada* stood for the rural areas. *Paura* stood for the people living in the urban areas and *Janapada* stood for the people living in rural areas. Hence, they were called *Paura* and *Janapada*.

But apart from these social and geographical units, the *arthashastra* of Kautilya, the *Jataka* stories and the *Mahabharata* also mention third unit of the state which was called frontier areas. This area was normally populated by the tribal population. These tribes were Nishads, Bhills, Shabaras, Pulindas and others. These forest areas were governed by the forest chieftains. Many of these tribes were in the hunting and food gathering stage of development. These tribes were well-organised, brave and acted in unison. They behaved like enemy at the time of emergency. (Bhattacharya, 2002: 147) Therefore, Kautilya pointed out that hostility of these tribes was more dangerous because the tribes lived in their own territory, they were many in number, they were brave and fight openly. They could capture a part of the country or ruin it because a forest chief had a potential to become independent king (Chousalkar, 1991: 43) Therefore, both in the

Arthashastra and the *Jatakas*, several examples are given of the revolts in the frontier areas of the state.

But it must be noted that all frontier areas of the state were not dominated by the tribal population as sometimes the area was dominated by a vassal or sometimes, the crown prince was appointed as the governor of that area. But it was accepted by the writers on the science of polity that the power of the king in the frontier areas was comparatively weak.

In the Shantiparva of the *Mahabharata*, there was discussion on methods of the integration of the tribal communities in the main body of the Indian society. The great epic mentioned a large number of tribes. King Mandhata asked Indra how to integrate these sections in the society ! (12.65.15) Indra advised Mandhata to bring them under his governance and gradually ask them to follow the principles of *Dharma* such as truth, compassion, non-violence and self-control. They should pursue the profession that they were following for their livelihood. They should perform sacrifices. (12.65.21) Thus, there was an attempt to bring them under the influence of Vedic culture but at the same time, they were allowed to follow their own traditional practices. It is the argument of Dr.V.S. Agrawala that this was the method normally followed to incorporate the tribal elements in the Indian society. (Agrawala, 1968: III 65)

Social Order in Ancient India

Indian society was divided in four Varnas- Brahmins, Kshatriyas, Vaishyas and Shudras. During the Vedic period, Vaishyas and Shudras were called 'Vish'. Political power was in the hands of Brahmins and Kshatriyas. The *Mahabharata* advocated close alliance of Brahmins and Kshatriyas. But the political power didn't always remain with the Kshatriyas as the great Magadh dynasties of Shishunag. Nanda and Maurya belonged to the Shudra caste. With the emergence of traders and other rich sections of the society, power got transferred to these sections of the society. The tribal chieftains and foreign invaders were brought in the mainstream of Indian society by the Brahmin priests as they furnished mythological *Pauranik* genealogies to claim that a particular king came from such a great dynasty. This was necessary to give them legitimacy. The Brahmins organised the ceremony of 'Hiranya garbha' to give rebirth to these kings as Kshatriyas. Dr D. D. Kosambi was of the opinion that several southern kings of tribal origin boasted that they had performed the golden womb ceremony to get rebirth. The priest chanted the mantras of child birth and pregnancy in order to signify new birth and new status of the king. Usually, these kings were given the status of Kshatriya Varna with the *gotra* of the Brahmin priest. Some of the medieval kings claimed Brahmin and Kshatriya status as it was done by the Satvahanas. (Kosambi, 1966: 171) Normally, kings married women of different castes and classes. Though there were caste differences but there did not seem to have intense caste antagonism during this period. The general nature of absorption of tribal communities in Indian society, allowing them to retain their tribal customs and the institutions, did not require use of force. Hence, changes in India took place with minimum use of force. (172)

But it wouldn't be correct to say that force or violent method was not used when the issue became political. The moment the tribal opposition assumed political form and threatened the dominance of the ruling class or existence of the state, the ancient Indian state used maximum force to put it down.

Population in ancient India was divided between the *Paura* and the *Janapada*. The *Paura* meant urban city dwellers or the citizens of the capital city and the *Janapada* stood for the people living in the rural areas. The leading elements from both the sections played an important role in political affairs of the state. Explaning their class background to Dr. Kosambi wrote; 'the *arthashastra* doesn't make caste as primary basis for classes. One prominent upper class was covered without specification of caste by the dual term- *Paura-Janapada*. The two are not completely antithetical designations for urban and rural citizens. For every *Janapada* had a city headquarters, every city its *Janapada* hinterland. The context makes it clear that they are not just residents. But propertied citizens who had strong following (presumably from tribal splinters), enjoyed special position with respect to the state and constituted public opinion."

(Kosambi, 1956: 223) Thus, the class of the *Paura* and *Janapada* was an important class that cut across caste lines in ancient India.

The Nature of State and the Concept of Oriental Despotism

During the *Janapada* phase, the state in ancient India was mainly divided between republics or *gana-Samgha* polity and monarchy. Ruling class of the state was called *gana* and the *Samgha* signified the state proper. Politically, the *gana-Samgha polity* was more homogenous because it was dominated by a single tribe or a group of tribes and it took its decisions by following the democratic methods. Monarchy always faced the danger of rebellion because the monarch ruled over more heterogeneous society and controlled a larger area of the country. But with the emergence of Maurya empire, the *gana-Samgha* polity suffered decline. It showed the signs of revival in the first few centuries of the Christian era but ultimately it was destroyed by the Gupta king Samudragupta. As a result, monarchy became the normal form of government in ancient India.

There was a gradual development of state in ancient India. The *Janpada* state during sixth and fifth centuries B. C. was smaller in size and it consisted of tribal population. But subsequently, these states assumed more complex form with larger areas under their control and heterogeneous population. The organisational structure of the government also became more complex as its functions grew. Agriculture, cattle breeding and trade became the main economic sources of state. *Janpada* states were replaced by the monarchies of the Nandas and Mauryas. The state during first millennium after the Christian era was large in size and it was ruled by monarchs. States were divided between the interior region and the outer areas. In the Mahabharata there is discussion on the organisation of the state. A village is a basic unit and 10 villages constitute second group. Third and fourth groups consist of 100 and 200 villages and the last groups of villages consists of 1000 villages. The fortified city is governed by a superintendent. (Banerji, 1976: 165)

Western scholars in nineteenth century, under the influence of Orientalism, expounded the concept of oriental despotism. It was their contention that despotism was a special feature of Asian societies and the Asian societies developed this peculiar form of government because of prevalence of Asiatic mode of production in these countries. These historians held that the Oriental societies didn't have robust sense of history because these societies didn't undergo basic social and political changes. As a result, for thousands of years, these societies remained static. The king was owner of property. Also, there prevailed communal ownership of property. Land was arid and it could be brought under the cultivation with the help of artificial irrigation which could be provided by constructing huge river based water works. According to Marx, the state played a more positive role in the Asiatic states and the Asiatic despotism was the result of complicity of passive, unresisting stratum of producers in virtually self-contained stagnant villages whose produce did not become commodity till it reached hands of state. (Kosambi, 1985: 90).

But now progressive research has shown that these opinions were not based on historical facts and the Indian society did undergo basic changes. Indian state didn't control all the activities of the society and there was right of property in ancient India. There was no communal ownership of property. Indians disliked despots. In fact, despotism was not the special character of either Eastern or Western societies because in the first and second millennium of the Christian era, Europe had produced more dreadful and ferocious despots than Asia. The Greek phase in the European history was an exception because during the Periclean Athens, perhaps the Athenians enjoyed unprecedented liberty, but this period of history cannot be generalised to claim that throughout history Europe was land of democracy and Asia was land of despotism.

In ancient India, political ideology of protest was advocated and an alternative path of politics was also discussed.

Ideology of Political Dissent in Ancient India

In ancient India, the Vedic ideology was considered as the dominant ideology and it developed religion of sacrifices and Varna based social order. In the sixth century B.C., there emerged different heterodox schools of thought which challenged the dominant Vedic ideology and put forward their own view point. They did not approve of religion of sacrifice which was based on violence and killing of animals. Four important schools of thought represented the ideology of dissent and these four schools of thought were the *Ajivikas*, Jainas, Lokayatas and the Buddhists. All of them repudiated the Vedic dogma.

Political ideology of Vedic state was evolved around performance of different sacrifices and it was assumed that the performance would bring manifold benefits to the sacrificer and to the people. It was also an important means to legitimise authority of king. The Vedic king was enjoined to perform horse sacrifice to expand his territory. The aggressive politics was justified by religious ceremony. Under the influence of the *Atharvan* rites, which recommended use of magic and incantations to destroy the power of the enemy, the kings performed sacrifices like 'Dying around the holy fire' to annihilate their enemies. (Zimmer, 1957) But this blatant use of incantations and violence against the animals was not appreciated by the new philosophies.

The philosophy of the *Ajivikas* which was expounded by Makkhali Gosala was an ascetic and pacifist philosophy. It believed in the efficacy of the destiny. Gosala held that human endeavours were the slaves of destiny. Following were four important principles of this school of thought – equanimity towards all creatures, absence of endeavour, truthful speech, complete disregard of action and indifference in seeking knowledge. (Agrawala, V. S., 1963: 393-94) He was called Manki in the Shantiparva. (12.171) In the epic, Manki held that he had decided not to strive after any object. He would develop universal friendliness, would hate none and would give trouble to no one. He would abuse no one but would return goodness to every one. He would be satisfied with whatever he had received and he would live peaceful life. (12.171)

According to Dr. A. L. Basham, Buddhism, Jainism and Ajvikism were reflections of the socio-political changes of that time. The *Ajivikas* believed in the order in the universe which they called Niyati or destiny. Gosala's theory was more appropriate to the single ruler, hence, his philosophy became popular when the Mauryas ruled the land single handedly (Basham, 2002: 286-87) But the greatest contribution of Gosala was his concept of equanimity and friendliness that dominated

Indian philosophy. The Vedic thinkers sought to domesticate the hidden power of destiny that laid in the performance of sacrifices to secure material pleasures, Gosala decided to live with destiny by following the Pacifist philosophy. Thus, he represented powerful dissent against the Vedic ideas of sacrifices. Violence and the desire to possess merit.

The Charvakas represented the second school of thought which questioned the efficacy of Vedic doctrines. They were opposed to performance of sacrifices and harshly criticised those who performed these rituals. In the *arthashastra*, Brihaspati a Lokayata teacher said, "The Vedic lore is only the cloak for one conversant with the ways of the world." (1.2-5) In the *Mahabharata*, a Lokayata Brahmin, who was a friend of Duryodhana came and accused Yudhishthira of immoral behaviour. He said that out of lust for power, he had killed his own clansmen and even teachers. He condemned his behaviour. Brahmins present there immediately attacked and killed him. (12.38-39) It was clear from this statement that the Charvakas were opposed to wars which were waged to capture political power. The Lokayata teachers did not approve of performance of Vedic rituals, dogma of *Varna* system and supremacy of Brahmins. They gave more importance to *artha* and *kama purusharthas* and exhorted the rulers to develop the sources of *artha*- that is aquiculture, trade and cattle breeding.

The Jains were supporters of non-violence and peace. Hence, they were opposed to Vedic religion and bloody sacrifices. They also rejected determinism of Gosala and pleaded for earnest striving for perfection as the goal of human beings. Non-violence was good for the society as well as it was good for salvation of the individual. Mahavira told the Jain monks that "in whatever house, village, city or region, he may be, if a monk is attacked by men of violence or suffers from any other hardship, he should bear it all like a hero. The saint, with true vision, conceives compassion for all the world. The great sage becomes a refuge for injured creatures, like an island which the waters cannot overwhelm." (De Bary, 1972: 68) The Jains were of the view that the method of peace was more desirable than war because war didn't solve problems of the world. (90) The Jain monk Hema-Chandra criticised the nature of political duties and blamed king's ministers for extorting money by force from others. In turn their master would extort money from them because they extorted everyone. (90-91) In the Acharang sutra the monks were advised to avoid travelling in countries which had non-monarchical polities.

In the Jain Puranas there is a story of two powerful brother kings- Bharat and Bahubali. There emerged conflict between the two and Bahubali humbled his brother but he realised that the path of violence and war was no good and hence, he abandoned it in the pursuit of *Dharma*.

Ideology of Dissent of Buddha

Gautam Buddha was opposed to the Vedic policy of violence in the sacrifices and the war model of horse sacrifices. He was opposed to the Vedic dogma of divine creation of social order and pleaded for social equality and compassion. Buddha put forward an alternative path of politics which was not based on violence and conflict but it was based on development of the land and reconciliation.

In the *Kootdanta* Sutra, Buddha had opposed the performance of Vedic sacrifices. According to him, there was a king who used to perform a number of sacrifices- throughout the year in which he sacrificed a large number of animals. He incurred a lot of expenses as he had to pay the fees to a large number of Brahmins. The slaves and workers were unhappy because they had to work ceaselessly during this period. Due to neglect of the duty, the kingdom was visited by robbery and brigandage as robbers plundered the people. Budhisattva as a minister to the king told him, "At present, there is no peace in your kingdom as villages and cities are plundered by robbers. In this situation, if you impose fresh taxes on the people, that will not be appreciated. You may follow the policy of punishing the robbers by putting them in jail, by banishing them from the kingdom or by putting them to death. But that would not solve the problem because there would be few more robbers to revolt against the king." He pointed out that this was not the right method of dealing with robbers. The correct method of overcoming the disturbances was to help those people who wanted to cultivate the land. He said, "You give the land, seeds and oxen to cultivators. Help these people with capital who want to get involved in trade and give the government jobs to those who want to serve in the government. Once the people got engaged in their work they liked, there would not be any revolts in the state and the people would happily pay their taxes and this would ensure alround prosperity for the people." (Kosambi, D., 2007: 244-45) For that purpose, he asked the king to discontinue all the wasteful sacrifices. The king followed the advice given by Buddha. Slowly, the conditions improved. Robbers got involved in their economic activities and as a result, brigandage stopped. There was increase in production. Both slaves and workers were happy as they did not have to do the hard work. Thus, there was prosperity in the state.

Buddha told the king that if he still wanted to perform the sacrifice, he should first obtain the permission of the people of his kingdom. After securing permission, he put down following conditions –

(1) King should not accept or give gifts to anybody in the sacrifice.

(2) No animal would be sacrificed. Only oil, butter and foodgrains would be used to give votive offerings.

(3) No trees would be cut in order to prepare big pandals for the function.

(4) Nobody, including slaves and workers would be forced to work in the sacrifices against their will.

(5) The rich people of the kingdom should not give any gifts to him but should invest the money for the gift for the welfare of the poor people of the kingdom. (246-47) Thus, by allowing the king to perform the sacrifices with these conditions, Buddha completely changed the nature of sacrifice.

Buddha was opposed to the war model of horse-sacrifice and the concept of conquest with the help of violence and war. He was also opposed to the peculiar school of *arthashastra* which was called *Kshatravidya* or the science of politics. Along with other philosophical schools, he opposed the teaching of teachers of political science. In the Maha Umagga *Jataka* (528) there is a story of *Kshatra Vidya Vadi* minister who said that for the king, fulfillment of his self-interest was the most desirable thing. In that pursuit, he could kill his close relatives, including parents, teachers and brothers, if they acted against his interests. At another place, the follower of *Kshatravidya* argued that one should save his disinterested self by following gentle or severe means at his disposal because for him, the survival was the most important thing. He could practice *dharma* after the emergency was over. (Ghoshal, 63-64) This advice was not acceptable to Buddha as he pointed out that it was wrong to follow the path of untruth to save one's own skin.

Buddha's Views on Politics

What were Buddha's views on politics? In a dialogue with Simha who was the *Senapati* of the Licchavi republic, he put forward his own viewpoint. Simha asked three questions to Buddha about nature of politics. His first question was –

(1) "I am a warrior and I am appointed to maintain law and order, wage wars against the enemies and punish the criminals. How should I perform these functions in the light of doctrine of non-violence?"

(2) "Buddha teaches the doctrine of complete self-surrender. Should I suffer the evil doer to do whatever he pleases and yield submissively to him?"

(3) "Does Buddha believe that the war which is waged in the righteous cause should be forbidden?"

Buddha gave answers to these important questions as follows –

(1) Buddha pointed out that he believed in philosophy of non-violence and argued that one shouldn't do injury to any one and be full of love and kindness. He pointed out that the one deserved punishment should be punished but he should be made to understand that he was punished for his own evil deeds and not because of the ill will of the people. The criminal should realise that he was punished for his crime. As soon as he realised it, punishment would purify his soul.

(2) Buddha taught complete surrender of self, but he did not preach surrender to the powers that were evil. The people should struggle against the evil because the struggle was a

part of life. Those who waged struggles to save self-interest and to achieve self-aggrandisement would get no rewards but those who struggled in the cause of truth and righteousness would get rewards.

(3) Buddha held that any warfare that involved killing of our brothers was lamentable but those people who waged righteous war after having exhausted all the means to preserve the peace were not to be blamed. He must be blamed who was the cause of a war. (Carus, P., 1972: 125-28) He further maintained that those Kshatriyas who went to war, should be prepared to lay down their life, for, that was the destiny of the warrior; but those Kshatriyas who had won the war, should understand instability of the earthly things and offer hand of friendship to his downtrodden enemy. He should say, "Come now and make peace and let us be brothers." In this way, he should gain victory yielding great rewards. (128) Therefore, his final advice to Simha was, "struggle then and fight your battles vigorously but as the soldier of truth and righteousness." (129). Here Buddha laid down three important principles of his alternative politics.

(1) A general can wage war against his unrighteous enemy after exhausting all avenues of maintaining peace. He shouldn't avoid war when it became inevitable.

(2) When he suffered defeat, he should valiantly lay down his life, but he should not surrender. But if he secured victory, he should propose treaty of peace and friendship to his defeated enemy.

(3) The struggle was a part of life but Buddha didn't approve struggles which were launched to serve self-interest of the king; but he appreciated the struggles which were waged to safeguard truth and righteousness. Thus, Buddha's politics was politics of dhamma. He stood for truth, non-violence and compassion and asked the people to struggle in the cause of *dharma*. He didn't want to fight evil with hatred but evil with goodness. He sought to change of enemy's heart to bring him to the side of truth and righteousness.

Thus, Buddha, Mahavira, Gosala and Charvaka represented ideological dissent to the dominant Vedic religion. They wanted to evolve the alternative path of politics by waging struggles against wrong tendencies and by putting forward alternative politics.

Fearlessness is Dharma

The *Dharmashastra-Smriti* tradition was opposed to the arbitrary behaviour of the kings. It is said that the temporal power of the king is supported by people as long as it follows the path of dharma and king looses his divinity and the right to obtain obedience of people if he became slave of passions. According to Dr. Coomarswami, an individual tyranny of a despot and his self importance leads to disintegration and death of body politic and ultimately self government depends on self-control. (Commarswami, A.K., 1978: 85-86) It is believed that dharma was based on "Samay" or the social contract and the king had promised to protect the life and property of the people. In return of that the people agreed to pay him one-sixth of his produce. The Mahabharata said that this was salary or 'Vetana' of the king. If he did not protect and became the slave of his passions, the people had right to overthrow him. The great epic advised the people to shun such a king like a leaky boat.(12.57.57)

It is argued that if king did not follow the path of dharma, he would suffer the consequences. It could be human as well as divine. In the *Jatakas* and the Mahabharata there are several examples of wicked kings being destroyed because of divine wrath. As far as human consequences are concerned the wicked and cruel kings were killed by their subjects; for example the Mahabharata says, "The subjects being united would kill that sinful and cruel king who does not protect, misappropriates money, destroys things and is not charitable. (Banerjee, 1976: 157) It says the king who is not charitable, of violent nature and gives sever punishments to subjects perishes.(157) It said the best of kings is he in whose territory people fearlessly move about like the sons moving about in the house of father." (161)

When king did not pursue the path of dharma and did not exercise self-control he suffered consequences. In the Panchatantra there is a story of a prodigious snake. The snake lived in the snake pit of a big tree and struck terror in the minds of the people. It moved about in a beaten track. One day it decided to leave beaten track and followed new path which was not smooth. It was full of thorns. As a result, the snake suffered injuries and some cuts to its body. While coming back the snake was attacked by thousands of ants. It killed many ants but ultimately the ants killed the snake. The Panchatantra declared, "beware of populace enraged, a crowd is a fearsome thing, the ants devoured the giant snake" (A. Ryder, 1972: 75) Moral of the story is that when king abandons path of dharma, he may invite wrath of people. Angry mob could destroy a more powerful king also. In the Mahabharata, it is said that the king who did not follow path of dharma and who struck terror in the minds of the people was a despot. He was a wolf in human form. (12.254)

In the Shantiparva of the great epic it is said that the essence of dharma was 'abhayatva' or fearlessness. Trader Tuladhara tells ascetic Jajali that the essence of dharma was non-violence, universal friendship and beneficence. One should not strike fear in the minds of the people. He should not fear others. Those who oppress and enslave others could never get true happiness. (12. 254) Fearlessness is the essence of dharma, and the Shantiparva tells that a person of pure heart and good character should not get scared of the wicked persons, thieves and king. (12.251)

Thus, in the non-Vedic and the Vedic schools of thought protest against unjust government is justified. It is argued that violence, injustice lack of self control and driving wedge between different groups of the people give birth to dissatisfaction and resentment of the people.

References

Agrawala, V. S. (1963), *India As It Knows to Panini,* Prithvi, Varanasi.

Agrawala, V.S. (1968), *Bharat-Savitri* in three volumes, Sasta Sahitya, Delhi.

Banerji, S. C. (1976), Indian society in the Mahabharata, (Based on Smriti material in the Mahabharata), Bharat-Manisha, Varanasi.

Basham, A. L. (2002), *History and Doctrines of the Ajivikas,* Motilal Banarassidass, Delhi.

Bardey De (Ed.) (1972), *Sources of Indian Tradition*, Motilal Banarasidas, Delhi.

Bhagvat, D. (1980), *Siddhartha Jataka,* Vol. I, Varada, Pune.

Bhattacharya, S. C. (2002), *Secular and Pluralistic Elements in the Idea of State in Early India*, Indian Institute of Advanced Study, Shimla.

Carus, P. (1972), *The Gospel of Buddha*, Tuckson Communications inc.

Chousalkar, A. (1991), *The Theory of Rebellion in the Politics of Aristotle and the Arthashastra of Kautilya*, Indological Book House, Delhi.

Ghoshal, U. N. (1966), *A History of Indian Political Ideas*, Oxford University Press, Mumbai.

Kangle, R. P. (1969), *Prachin Bharatiya Rajniti,* Mauj Prakashan, Mumbai.

Kosambi, D. D. (1985), *History and society-problems of interpretation,* University of Mumbai, Mumbai.

Kosambi, D. D. (1975), *Culture and Civilisation of Ancient India*; an outline, Vikas, Delhi.

Mishra, S. (1973), *Janapada States in Ancient India*, Bharatiya Vidya, Varanasi.

Rydcr, A. (1972), *The Panchatantra,* Jaico Publications, Mumbai.

Chapter – IV

Forms of Political Protest in Early India

In ancient India the state underwent considerable change. During the Vedic period there was kingship and in the post-Vedic period only the state began to assume territorial form. Slowly small *Janapada* states were replaced by 16 *Mahajanpadas* during sixth century B. C. With the emergence of Kosala and Magadha states, days of the *Janapada* states were over. The *Mahajanapadas* were replaced by the empires of the Nandas and the Mauryas. In the first century A.D. on the ruins of the Mauryan empire, numerous successor states emerged but none could achieve strength and spread of the Mauryan empire. In this chapter different forms of political protest and revolts will be examined with the help of Kautilyan Arthashastra, the Mahabharata, the Ramayana, the Dharmashastras and the *Jatakas*. Though the *Jatakas* were written in the sixth century A. D. they represented social and political life of earlier period. The state referred to in these texts is not empire.

Political Protest in the Vedic Literature

During the Vedic period the state was of a small rize and it had not yet developed its constituent elements. At that time, kingship was elective and the *Sabha* and the *Samiti* were two powerful popular bodies. The *Samiti* was a body of the whole people and it was sovereign body. Hence, the king prayed that *Sabha* and *Samiti* were two daughters of Prajapati and they should bestow favour on him. (Kangle, 1969: 32) It is said that the *Samiti* had a right to depose and exile king. Therefore, the king had to follow advice of the *Samiti.* (Pande, 83)

There are several examples of removal of the king by the people. According to the *Shatapatha Brahmana*, king Paunsayana was removed by the people. Similarly the Srinjayas deposed their king. (Roychoudhari, 1925: 157) Sarvadaman Bharat-son of Dushyanta and Shakuntala was also removed because of his misrule. According to Dr. Saletore Aparuddha and Arajata were two technical terms used in ancient India. Aparuddha means expulsion of kings from their realms and their efforts to regain lost kingdom. Arajata means kingless state or anarchy. (Saletore, (1971: 131)

Savitri's father in law Dyumatsen was removed from power and exiled to jungle. Kings performed *Sautramani* sacrifice to secure their lost kingdom. (Panday, 63)

The Sautramani Sacrifice

During the Vedic period, kings performed different sacrifices to propitiate gods. Some of these sacrifices were performed to destroy enemies of the king and in the *Atharva Veda* there is a mention of such *Atharvan* and the *Angira* practices. The sacrifice is called *Sautramani* was performed by the Kshatriyas to secure victory in war and by the Vaishyas to acquire wealth. The deported or the exiled kings performed it to secure his lost kingship (Pandey, 63). Originally this sacrifice was performed by Indra to cure him of over indulgence in Soma. Deported king performed it and prayed to gods that Indra would come back to friendly relations with people. The priest will chant the songs and apply the *Sautramani* to king's restoration. In the *Atharva Veda* the king prayed that those kings men and strangers who opposed him, would drive away and he would be restored to kingdom. (Atharva Veda, Vol. 5, 112)

In the Atharva Veda, the procedure of the ritual of restoration of the deposed king is described and the title of the Mantra is 'swarajye Rajyan Punha Sthapanam' 'स्वराज्ये राज्यं पुनःस्थापनम्'. There are six *mantras* invoking the support of different gods for restoration of the exiled king. Following are three important *mantras*:

(1) Blessings of the god of fire are invoked to bring the king back to the country who has acquired qualities of a *Kshatriya*.

(2) Blessings of the god Varuna are invoked and the king is asked to quickly return to his realm and among his subjects because the people want him to come back.

(3) Blessings of brothers Ashvini Kumar and Indra are invoked to tell the king that his erstwhile enemies are also inviting him and the people had chosen him as the king. No one should oppose his return as king. Let all agree to bring king back to his realm. (The Atharva Veda, 3.3-6).

Thus the king is restored back to his throne (Agrawala-Vol. III, 109-110) According Prof. B. A. Saletore, the Srinjayas expelled their king Dushtakratu from their kingdom. They also exiled the sage Rivottras Patava Sthapati along with him. Subsequently, Sthapati performed '*Sautramani*' sacrifice for the king and reinstated him to his throne, Saletore, 1971: 132)

There are '*abhyudaya*' and '*Abbichara*' practices in the Atharva-Veda. As far as *Abhyudaya* practices are concerned the priests performed prayers to secure harmony and reconciliation among the people. He prays "unity of hearts and unity of minds freedom from hatred do I procure for you." (the Atharva Veda, III 30, 134) There are charms to secure harmony, allay discord and against strife and bloodshed. The *Abhichara* practices or black magic is used against enemy.

With gradual development of the society, the influence of magic and the black magic declined and the people realised that meaningful popular intervention was needed to fight tyranny and injustice.

Political Protest in the Buddhist Literature

Gautam Buddha decided to follow the path of righteousness. There was a conflict between the Shakyas and the Kolias about distribution of water of river Rohini. Young Siddhartha wanted to resolve it peacefully but the Shakya assembly passed a resolution in favour of war with the Koliyas. They told Siddhartha that he should give consent to the resolution or to leave the Shakya gan-Samgha. Siddhartha decided to leave the state in protest against the decision.

Forms of Political Protest in the *Jatakas*

The *Jatakas* formed an important piece of literature on Buddhism. There are three boxes of literature- which are called Tripitikas. They are Suttanipata, Vinaya Pitaka and Abhidhamma Pitaka. In the Suttanipata are included Digha Nikaya, Mazzim, Samyutta and Anguttara, Nikayas. Khuddak Nikay is the firth part of it and the *Jatakas*, the Dhammapada are part of the Khuddak Nikay (Bhagvat, 1975: I-3) It is the opinion of the scholars that the *Jatakas* that are available today are last composed in the fifth century A.D. but they represent the conditions that prevailed in fifth century B.C. There are total 550 *Jataka* stories and some of them are very small and some of them like Maha Umagga *Jataka* are very long. In these stories, importance of the principle of righteousness is constantly stressed.

In the Tandulanali *Jataka* (No. 5), there is a story of an avaricious king who unilaterally decided to increase the prices of foodgrains because his dishonest minister asked him to do so. But this corrupt minister was exposed by Bodhisattva. The minister fixed the price of 500 horses as a pint of rice after taking bribe from the foreign trader. Bodhisattva showed that the minister was dishonest. The people started laughing at the king. As a result, he had to sack the dishonest minister.

In the Kula Vaka *Jataka* (No. 31), story of Magha was narrated. Magha lived in a village. He collected 30 families. They decided to work together and help people. They collectively worked hard to construct roads, wells, started schools, constructed bridges, tanks and rest houses for the people. As a result, there were no conflicts among the people. This was not liked by the village chief or the Gramabhojaka who used to take bribes from the people. Now the people refused to pay him bribes. Hence, he complained to the king and told him that these 30 robbers were looting the country. There was no peace in the country and the people refused to pay taxes. Magha and his friends were brought in the capital. Without making any inquiry the king ordered that they should be executed. Magha told them that they should not hate their tormenters but to have feeling of love towards all. The elephants refused to crush Magha and his friends under the feet. The king realised his mistake and withdrew his order. He made inquiry about the conditions in the country and saw that there was all-round development.

In the Sammodman *Jataka* (No. 33), the birds resolved to unite and fly together if they were caught in a net of hunter. They succeeded in doing this due to their unity and strength, but due to rivalry, jealousy and quarrels, the division took place among them and next time, when the hunter spread his net, there was no united action from the birds. As a result, they were all caught and killed by the hunter. The unity of the people could only help them fight against enemy was the moral of story. In the Tayyodhamma *Jataka* (No. 38) young monkey prince foiled wicked design of his father to kill him with the help of his friends and intelligence.

In the Sachhaankir *Jataka* (78), there is a story of wicked prince. When he was in danger he was saved by his friend. The prince became king, when his friend came to meet him the king wanted to execute him on the trumped up charges. At that time, the prince was riding on the elephant and the servants were beating the hapless friend. But he did not lose the stability of his mind. When the people asked him about the cause of the punishment, he told the people that once he had saved the life of the king, but now he wanted to kill him. The moment the people came to know about evil designs of king, the Brahmins, Kshatriyas and other people got enraged. They came together and attacked the king who was sitting on the elephant. He was pulled down and killed by the mob. His body was thrown in the ditch and the young Bodhisattva (old friend of the king) was anointed as the king. Thus, in this story, the people enraged by the evil nature of king, came together and lynched him.

In the Telepatta *Jataka* (No. 96), the king of Gandhara came under the influence of a beautiful celestial girl who asked the king to give his kingdom to her. He said that he did not have control over all the people, but he would give the control of the palace to her. She was a goblin. She ate away all inhabitants of the palace including the king! After her departure, all the ministers and citizens of the country came together and elected Bodhisativa as their king.

In the Asatrupa *Jataka* (100), there was a story of the prince of Varanasi. His kingdom was attacked by the enemy who killed his father and married his mother. The young prince succeeded in beating safe retreat. Subsequently, he gathered forces and attacked the city. His mother clandestinely advised him that he should encircle the city and impose blockade on the city for seven days. He imposed blockade. Due to this blockade, the people didn't get milk, food and water and they suffered no end. As a result, the enraged citizens, attacked and assassinated the king. The Prince was anointed as the king of Varanasi.

In the Ekpanna *Jataka* (149), there was a story of wicked Lichchavi prince who was a slave of anger and devoid of any compassion. He used to give very harsh punishments. He was yet to become the king. Bodhisattva was his friend. He told him that the people even uprooted small creeper if it tasted bitter. They would kill him if continued to follow cruel and harsh policy. He waned him that the people wouldn't offer kingship to him or they would banish him from the kingdom or they would lynch him, if he did not mend his ways. Therefore, he advised him to follow the principles of peace, friendship and compassion. The prince accepted his advise and behaved accordingly.

In the Manichor *Jataka* (194), the king of Varanasi wanted to marry a beautiful wife of his Purohita. Hence, he decided to implicate the Purohit in a false case of the theft of Jewels. He was arrested and the king issued the order that he should be executed. His wife Sujata prayed to god Indra to intervene and save her husband. God intervened and killed the evil king. The people rejoiced at this divine intervention and annoinated Bodhisattva as the king. In the Mahapingala *Jataka* (240), there is a story of king Pingala who was very wicked. He exploited the people. Bodhisattva was born as his son. He showed no mercy to his own relatives. He ruled over the kingdom for many years and died. When he died, the people rejoiced at his death and anointed Bodhisattva as the king.

In the Vaddaki Sukar *Jataka* (283), there is a story of pigs who got scared of tiger. A powerful pig united all the pigs under his leadership and unitedly attacked and killed the tiger. The real enemy of the pigs was a wicked ascetic who incited the tiger. Hence, the pigs attacked the ascetic and killed him.

In the Siri *Jataka* (284), the war was won despite the fact that the king was killed in the war because of expertise of Bodhisattva, hence, he was elected as the king after the victory.

In the Khantivadi *Jataka* (313), there is a story of a wicked king. Bodhisattva was born as an ascetic. He claimed that he was a supporter of peace, compassion and tolerance. Therefore, he was tormented and tortured by the wicked king, but he didn't show any hatred and suffered the death in the spirit of equanimity. The wicked king met with divine punishment as he was devoured by earth and engulfed by the fire. In the Chulladhammapal *Jataka* (358) a wicked king mercilessly killed his child son and as a result he met divine retribution.

In the Darimukha *Jataka* (378), Bodhisattva was elected as the king by the people because of the king of the country was dead. In the Pad Kushal *Jataka* (432), there is a story of the king who conspired to commit theft in his own palace to test the ability of Bodhisattva to apprehend thieves. Bodhisativa correctly spotted the thief. He declared that it was the purohita and the king who plundered the country. When the people came to know about it, the enraged people took sticks and weapons in their hands and killed the king and his purohita. They anointed Bodhisattva as the king.

In the Matanga *Jataka* (497), there is a story of revenge of the Brahmins against Bodhisattva who was born in a Matanga family. Bodhisattva acquired knowledge and he became famous as the pundit. The Brahmins didn't like this lower class pundit enjoying such popularity. He practiced *dharma*. Brahmins incited the king of the Mezha country who asked the servants to kill the pundit. The Pundit was killed. But because of this injustice, gods became angry and they burnt Mejz king to death and destroyed his kingdom completely.

In the Ganda Tinduka *Jataka* (520), there was a story of the king who unjustly levied taxes upon the people. Bodhisattva was a tree god. He went to the king and told him that he was governing kingdom unjustly. He should mend his ways. The king wanted to know the truth and he went to jungle to know what the people thought of his government. All the people he met abused the king of misgovernment, they said that the people were not happy because he levied heavy taxes on them. But the kingdom was not properly protected and the property of the people was plundered and thieves looted the people. They said that the evil king gave birth to evil people. The king decided to change his ways and governed the state justly.

In different stories, the jealous kings tried to kill their friends, sons, brothers, and ministers because they suspected that they would usurp their throne. (No. 539, 542)

In the Mahasutsoma *Jataka* (537) there is a story of Cannibal king who developed taste for eating human flesh. He started killing his own people. When the people came to know about it, they gathered outside the palace of the king and asked him to either leave this habit or leave the kingdom. The *Senapati* and ministers tried to convince him. But instead of changing habit, the king decided to leave kingdom. The king was exiled to jungle. Subsequently, Bodhisattva helped him change his habit.

The Vessantar Jataka

There is a story of a prince who donated the white elephant of the kingdom to a Brahmin. Knowing this people of the city got angry and demanded that the prince should he exiled. The king accepted the demand and sent the prince to jungle. He and his wife lived in the jungle. After some years the king came to know about the hard life his son was living. He called meeting of the people took their permission and brought back the prince and his wife. (Kosambi, D., 2007: 20-29)

In the Deeghati Kosal Jataka, Deerghau, whose father's kingdom was captured by the king of Kashi and his parents were murdered. While dying, his father told him that he should not nurse feeling of revenge against the enemy because emenity breeds enemity and cycle of revenge continues. Deerghau went to jungle, acquired knowledge and managed to get job in the king's palace. He got an opportunity to kill the king of Kashi but remembered his father's words and decided to bury enemity. He proposed peace. The king of Kashi agreed to his proposal and made him the king of Kosal. (Kosambi, D., 1979: 229-345)

We have studied the *Jataka* stories and tried to find out the forms of protest that the people followed against the despotic rulers.

The stories of Vessantar, Magha and Deerghau tell us that the Buddhist doctrines of non-violence, non-injury and the universal brotherhood found echo there. Vessantar willingly suffered forest life for his values. Notable fact is that the king had to follow the dictates of the people for expelling Vessantara out of town or for admitting him to the city. Both father and son did not go against the wishes of the people. Similarly, Deerghau could have killed the king but he did not do so because he wanted to terminate the cycle of enemity and revenge. This was consistent with Buddhist doctrine that one should try to fight the evil and after overcoming it, he should offer hand of friendship, Buddha always favoured peaceful reconciliation. Magha followed the path of doing constructive work to neutralise the evil and displayed no ill will towards his tormenters.

Protest in the Arthashastra of Kautilya

The Arthashastra of Kautilya contains a lot of information about the rebellion. (Chousalkar, 1991) Normally he did not favour the regicide because he was a supporter of monarchy. But he knew that if the ruler became a slave of passions and misbehaved with the people, he invariably incurred their wrath. As a result, he had to save either his kingdom or life.

Kautilya said that rebellion or revolt of the people can be called 'Prakriti kopa'. Prakriti means seven constituent elements of the state and 'kopa' means anger, disaffection or the wrath of the people. Apart from king, ministers, fort, army, treasury, rural areas and allies are the constituent elements and when these elements especially ministers, army, people living in the rural and urban areas and the ally get disaffected that is called 'Prakriti Kopa'. While defining Prakriti kopa, he wrote "Immoderation such as passion and so on rouses one's own constituents and wrong policy rouses enemies of the king to move against him. Both these amount to the demonical behaviour. The change in one's own people is caused rebellion". (Arthashastra, 9-7-1-3) He said "svajana vikar kopa" when there was change in the minds of the people against the king the revolts and protests would take place.

Kautilya said that there were two types of revolts- revolt in the interior and the revolt in the outer regions of the state. The first revolt took place in the capital city and the second in the rural areas or in the frontier regions. When the king became a slave of passions and lacked self control, that aroused anger of the people and got killed.

Kautilya said that rebellion or rebellious mood of the people could be called calamity befalling the state. He was of the view that the vices of the kings could be divided into two vices arising from personal behaviour of king and wrong policy.

Causes of Revolts

Kautilya first discussed the causes of revolt which resulted from the personal behaviour of the king. He said that the people got angry with the king if he became slave of his passions. He held that absence of training in lores was the cause of man's vices because untrained person didn't see fault in vices. He divided vices into two and held that a group of three vices sprang from anger and a group of four vices sprang from lust. Of the two-anger was more serious because it acted every-where and mostly, the kings who acted under the influence of anger were known to have been killed by risings among the subjects and those under the influence of lust were known to be killed by enemies and diseases as a result of losses. (8.3.5-7)

He didn't agree with Bharadvaja about efficacy of anger and held that it never brought good results. He wrote, "Becoming hated, making enemies and association with pain is anger. Humiliation, loss of wealth and association with harmful persons like thieves, gamblers, hunters, singers, players of instrument that is lust. Of these, being hated is a greater evil than humiliation, one being humiliated is held in their power by his own people and by others, the hated one is exterminated. Making enemy is a greater evil than loss of wealth. Loss of wealth endangers the treasury; making enemy endangers life. Association with a pain is a greater evil than association with harmful persons. Association with harmful persons can be remedied in a moment, association with pain causes prolonged duress, verbal injury, violation of property and physical injury are vices springing from anger." (8.3.13-23). According to Kautilya, violation of property meant loss of livelihood. Physical injury was more dangerous than the violation of property because even for a very large sum of money no one would desire loss of his life. Through physical injury a person incurred the same danger at the hands of others (8.2.27-29 and 34-35).

According to Kautilya, the group of four vices springing from lust, hunting, gambling, women and drink. He held that ultimately all these vices were dangerous. Hence he wrote, "lust means favouring of evil persons, anger, the suppression of good persons. Because of multitude of evils resulting from both of them are held to be a calamity without end." (8.3.65-66).

Kautilya had given several examples from history to show that the kings who didn't have control over their senses lost their kingdom as well as their lives. King Dandakya perished because of lust; Janmejaya perished because of anger, Aila perished because of extortion of money from all four Varnas. Ravana and Duryodhana lost because of excessive desire for possession of things that did not belong to them. Haihaya Arjuna perished because of arrogance and Vatapi and the Vrishnis perished because of their foolhardiness. (1.6.4-10).

All the vices of hunting, gambling, wine and women were bad but from the political point of view, Kautilya was of the view that gambling was the worst because it was the cause of civil strife. He wrote, 'The success or failure of one side, due to the stakes leads to strife among the subjects by creating two factions concerning animate and inanimate objects in particular in case of oligarchies and royal families there are dissensions caused by that. It is the most evil among the vices, as it favours evil men and it leads to weakness in administration". (8.3.62-64).

Though Kautilya was not a supporter of regicide, he saw the inevitability of assassination of the king, if he became a slave of six enemies of the senses. Normally, the revolt against the personal behaviour of the king might take place in the interior because the important people in the interior were adversely affected by it. This type of revolts might be supported by a large number of people from the urban areas as well as from countryside. In this case, his righteousness was important but then the righteous king would never become a slave of passions.

Meaning of 'Prakriti Kopa'

The rebellion or 'Prakriti Kopa' also meant the wrath of different constituent elements of the state. Revolts by ministers, the people from urban areas and countryside and army came under this. These elements got disaffected and became rebellious because of wrong policies of the king or instigation by the enemy. The role of enemy in instigating rebellion was important because it was in fact an application of expedient of dissension. He knew that the surest way of creating problem for the enemy was to stir rebellion in his territory. Rebellious and disloyal ministers were the great danger to the king, hence, he asked him to conduct loyalty tests of these before confirming their appointment (1.10. 1-20). Kautilya pointed out some causes of revolt and held that the harassment of the people by royal army or by royal officers, levying of excessive taxes on the people, king's inability to providing protection to the people from the attacks of robbers and forest tribes, lack of sources of livelihood, and the people stricken by famine were the causes of rebellion (7.4.7). He pointed out that disaffection, greed, harassment and impoverishment of the subjects either caused rebellion, or it invited the enemy's attacks.

In a long passage, which included all the causes of rebellion, Kautilya argued, "when the king discards good people and favours wicked, starts unrighteous practices and discontinues customary practices that are righteous, indulges in impiety and suppresses peity, punishes those who do not deserve punishment and doesn't punish those who deserve punishment, arrests good persons and doesn't arrest those who ought to be arrested, doesn't protect the subjects from thieves and robs them himself by ruining human exertion, by spoiling the excellences of work done, by doing harm to principal men, by dishonouring those who are worthy of honour, by opposing the elders. When king takes recourse to falsehood and partiality, by not requiring what is done and by not carrying out what is settled through the negligence and indolence of the king and because of destruction of well-being. Through these cause decline, greed and disaffection among the subjects." (7.5.19-26).

Kautilya held that impoverishment, greed and disaffection were the causes of rebellion. He was of the view that the subjects, when impoverished became greedy, when greedy they became disaffected and when disaffected, they either went over to the enemy or themselves killed the master. Therefore, the king should not allow these causes of decline, greed and disaffection among the subjects to arise, or if arisen, he should immediately counteract them (7.5.27-28). While discussing the dangers emanating from these sources, Kautilya held that ultimately they led to the rebellion of the people.

He maintained that the impoverished and greedy subjects were less dangerous than rebellious subjects because impoverished and greedy subjects when devoted to their master, remained steadfast in what was beneficial to the master or made the instigations futile (7.5.14-15). He wrote, "The impoverished through fear of harassment or extermination, prefer an immediate peace, fight or flight. The greedy, dissatisfied because of greed, willingly respond to the enemy's instigations. The disaffected rise in revolt when there is an enemy attack." (7.5.29-32)

The type of revolts and calamities we discussed ensued from the wrong policy of the king. Rebellions could also take place due to bad luck.

Kautilya was of the opinion that along with wrong policy, bad luck was also responsible for calamities. He held that fire, floods, disease, famine and epidemic were visitations from gods. He held floods more dangerous than fire because fire at best could burn a village or a half a village, but floods on the other hand, carried away hundreds of villages. Famines were more dangerous than disease because disease could affect only one region, but famine afflicted whole country and led to absence of livelihood. (8.4.1-6)

He was of the opinion that the natural calamities such as fire, floods were caused by providence and they should be overcome through prostration before gods and Brahmins. When there was excessive rain or drought or demonic creations, the means to overcome them were the rites prescribed in the 'Atharvaveda' and undertakings by holy men (1.7.82-84).

Four Groups of Rebells

Kautilya pointed out that the revolts were led by different group of persons because they were adversely affected by the policies of the king. He was of the view that the three classes of people- impoverished, greedy and disaffected get rebellious. He held that in the interior, ministers, royal chaplain, crown prince and commander-in-chief could become rebellious and in the outer regions, chief of countryside, forest chieftain, chief of tribes or the vassal could become rebellious. These people might exploit the favourable situation to stir trouble against the king.

He pointed out that there were four types of people who would take part in revolt against the king. They were enraged, greedy, frightened and proud people. He said that the enraged person was "one who is cheated after being promised certain things, of two persons equally skilled in some art or useful service, the one who is humiliated, one who is in disfavour because of a favourite of king, one who is defeated after being challenged to a contest, one who is distressed by banishment, one who hasn't achieved his object after incurring expenditure, one who is hindered from doing his duty or receiving his inheritance, one deprived of honour or office, one held back by members of the family, one whose women folk are molested by force, one who is put in prison, one who is fined after losing his suit in the court, one prevented from indulging in wrong conduct, one whose entire property is confiscated, one tormented in confinement, one whose kinsmen are exiled or killed – this is the group of enraged." (1.14.2) According to him, frightened meant "one who has himself thwarted some one. One who has committed serious wrong, one who has become known for sinful act, one frightened by punishment, meted out to another with a like offence, one who has seized some one's land, one who is subdued by force, one in any department who has suddenly amassed wealth, one hoping for a pretender from the king's family coming to the throne, one disliked by the king and one who entertains hostility towards the king. This is the group of the frightened." (1.14.3)

While describing the greedy, he said, "one who is impoverished, one whose property is taken by another, a miser, one in a calamity (or indulging in vice) and one indulging in rash transaction – this is the group of the greedy" and 'one who is filled with self-conceit, one desirous of honour, one resentful of honour done to his enemy, one placed in low position, one fiery in temper, one given to violence and one dissatisfied with his emoluments – this is the group of proud". (1.14.4-5)

These four groups of people might take part in rebellion because of their anger, greed, fear and self-conceit. The king should be aware of these elements and see to it that they were properly tackled. These types of people could be found among those who rose in revolt both in interior and outer regions.

Kautilya talked about the revolts in the rear as well as in the front side of the kingdom. He held that there was likelihood of uprising against the king if he had gone on expedition. Small disturbance in the rear was more dangerous because when the king had gone on expedition, treasonable men, enemies and foresters augmented the small disturbance all sides. This might incite some of constituents like ministers to rise against the king. If this happened, servants, allies, losses and expenses ate up whatever large gains obtained. Hence, he quoted a saying in the people that "misfortunes indeed have the mouth of a needle' because in the beginning uprising in the rear might look small but it had a potential to become a big threat because the disgruntled elements in the rear would exploit it to the hilt (9.3.3-4).

Thus, Kautilya's views on political protest were influenced by his concern for the security of the state. He agreed with other thinkers that anger and lust of the king invited wrath of the people and such kings were killed by the people. But as a serious student of politics he was aware of the fact that the king weakened by the disaffection of the people could easily become prey of the ambitious elements from the interior areas and outer regions because they sought to take advantage of the difficult situation. He knew that revolt of the people was not a spontaneous action and some amount of preparation and organisation was needed for it and it was done by the hostile ministers crown prince or the royal priest.

Forms of Protest in the *Mahabharata*

In the *Mahabharata*, we have several examples of how the people in India fought against the despots. The revolts of the people were either led by the ministers, ascetics, sages, neighbouring princes or common people. The epic talked about two types of revolts- the revolt in the interior and the revolt in the outer regions (12.82). It considered the revolt in the interior more dangerous.

One of the good examples of killing of a despot was that of killing of Kamsa by Krishna. Kamsa usurped throne of his father, imprisoned his sister Devaki and wanted to kill all the children of Devaki. Krishna and his brother Balrama were secretly brought up by Nanda. They came to Mathura on the invitation of Kamsa who plotted to kill them. Though both of them were young, they enjoyed tremendous popularity. Balrama killed two gladiators – Mushtika and Chanura who were asked to kill Krishna. Krishna attacked Kamsa and killed him on the spot. Assassination of Kamsa was rejoiced by the people. Old king Ugrasena was released from the jail and the chiefship was restored to him. The Harivamsha points out that Kamsa was unpopular with the subjects as he levied heavy taxes and the people feared him because of lack of self control. Hence, Krishna told Ugrasena that Kamsa was a stigma on the Yadav clan as he terrified the people. Hence, in the public interest, he had killed him. (More, 1995: 51-52)

In the Ghata *Jataka* (454) there is a Buddhist version of the story of Krishna. The *Jataka* described how both the wrestlers and Kamsa and his brother Upakamsa were killed by Balrama and Krishna.

The second story of killing the despots in the great epic was that of killing of the Haihaya king Sahasra Arjun by Parashurama.

Parashurama took the revenge of killing of his father and mother by the Haihaya king. Then, we have a story of king Vena who was killed by the sages because he became a slave of passions and started oppressing the people. (12.59)

In the *Mahabharata* the king was asked to pursue the path of *Dharma* and he should control his senses. The relationship between the king and the people was governed by 'Samaya' or contract. It is said that the king who did not protect the subjects, after making a contract was a thief because he received the salary for the same in the form of taxes. It was his duty to make good the property to the owners which was stolen by the thieves and which was not restored by the king. (12.76) (12.137) therefore, sage Vamadeo told the king that if he didn't follow the principles of *dharma*, he would be perished along with his family. (12-94)

The *Mahabharata* did not think that the king should not be punished for their wrong doing. There were many examples of regicide in the great epic. Therefore, in the celebrated statement in the *Anushasana parva*, Bhishma justified regicide and said, 'that king is more dead than alive in whose kingdom women are easily abducted from the midst of husbands and sons uttering cries and groans of indignation and grief. The subjects should arm themselves for slaying that king who does not protect them, who simply plunders their wealth, who confounds all distinctions, who is incapable of taking their lead, who is without compassion and regarded as the most sinful of kings. The king who tells the people that he is their protector, who does not or unable to protect them, should be slain by his subjects, like a mad dog is killed." (13.60, 31-33)

Agreeing with the Arthashatra, the *Mahabharata* held that the kings turned tyrants because of following factors:

(1) When the kings lose control over senses and aspires to confiscate others property.

(2) When kings impose heavy taxes on the people.

(3) When the kings punish the innocent people and do not punish those who deserved punishment.

(4) When the kings spoke in harsh language, insulted people and tried to take away wives of the people.

Protest in the Ramayana

In the Ramayana the problem of protest was discussed. When Dashrath, on the insistence of Kaikayi asked Kama to go on exile for 14 years, the people of Ayodhya protested against his decision. But Ramchandra asked the people to accept the king's decision. They wanted to accompany Rama to forest, wanted to migrate but Rama persuaded them not to do so.

Rama went to forest and his brother Bharat came to take him back to Ayodhya. He wanted to anoint him as the king. He told Rama that he would offer dharana in front of Rama like the Brahmins, who offered dharana and refused to leave the place until their demand was fulfilled. Rama told Bharata that he had no right to offer dharna because he had committed no offence! offering dharna and sleeping on the one side of the body was a very dangerous vow and Bharat should not do so. Again offering the dharana was a right of the Brahmins and as a Kshatriya Bharat had no right to do so. (the Ramayana, Vol. II-110)

Thus, in the Ramayana, Ram referred to ancient practice of Brahmins to perform agitation in the form of dharana to press for their demands. They used to sleep on the one side of the body on the road to create obstacles to the people.

The Brahmins during the tenth and eleventh centuries A.D. adopted this form of agitation against the kings and we have few examples of such agitators in the *Rajtarangini* of Kalhana.

Forms of Protest in the early India

In the *Jatakas* and the *Mahabharata*, there is discussion on the methods followed by the people to resist the unjust rule. Following were some of the methods:

(1) During the Vedic period, the method of performing Sautramani sacrifices was used to bring about change in the government.

(2) The kings were advised by the people and their friends not to follow the path of unrighteousness because ultimately, it brings down the government. If the king mended his way, we could see the improvement in the conditions. Also, the people would go to the king and request him not to punish those who were not guilty.

(3) The people- the *Paura* and *Janapada* from the cities and rural areas would come together and organise peaceful demonstrations against the policy of the unjust king. If he did not mend the ways, he was exiled from the kingdom.

(4) If there was no change in the behaviour of the king and if he continued to oppress the people, the people would gather together, take up arms in their hands, encircle and kill the king as advised by the Anushasana parva of the *Mahabharata*. A powerful king also cannot save himself if he was attacked by the enraged population as pointed by the *Panchatantra*.

(5) The people took recourse to mass migration if there was no way out. The mass migration would depopulate the country and it would adversely affect finances of the state.

(6) The people refused to pay taxes to the king because of his non-performance of duties and plundering by the robbers.

(7) Many times, the revolts were led by the close relatives of the king or by the ministers of the king and once they succeeded in overthrowing his power, they themselves became the king.

(8) After the killing of the despot, the people normally made his son or a brother the king but if there was no succession line available, they elected the king from among themselves as they didn't want to leave kingdom without king.

(9) Normally, there were revolts of the people in the frontier areas because they were populated by the hostile tribal chieftains. Sometimes, they gave shelter to the rebels and sometimes their help was sought to overthrow existing government. The help of Parvataka was taken by Chandragupta Maurya to overthrow the Nanda rule.

(10) The Indians believed that the unjust king would meet his *nemesis* at the hands of his own subjects, but if he escaped that punishment, he was bound to face divine retribution. He would be destroyed by the divine intervention. There are several stories in the *Jatakas* which clearly point out that despots were ultimately killed by gods and even if they were not killed by gods, they would go to hell and suffer consequences of their wickedness.

(11) Sometimes, the unjust behaviour of the king forced the people to invite just and virtuous king of the neighbouring state to intervene and to end despotic and unjust rule of the king.

Gautam Buddha put forward an alternative path of behaviour so that the people could follow it. In the *Magha Jataka*, Magha pursued the alternative path of politics and boldly faced its consequences. In the *Kootdanta* Sutra, he pointed out that robberies and dissidence of the people could not be overcome with the help of force, but it was to be overcome with the help of the policy of development which would give space to the people to chart out new path of life. He did not favour the path of violence but he did allow his followers to fight war in the cause of truth and righteousness.

In the political protest, class and caste played an important role because unless the revolt was supported by the powerful class of people, it did not have chances of success. At some places, the *Jatakas* clearly mentioned that *Paura-Janapada* took part in the mass action. At some places, it had mentioned Brahmans, Kshatriyas and the people. Secondly, leadership to these revolts was normally provided by someone who was close to the royal family, King's ministers or a person from Brahmin and Kshatriya castes. For example, Vena was killed by sages and Kamsa was killed by Krishna, Haihaya Arjuna was killed by Parashurama. In the Matanga *Jataka*, there was a clear case of caste antagonism when the king killed Matang Pandit because of Brahmin antipathy to him. The king and the people suffered divine retribution. In the *Kootdanta* Sutra, slaves and the workers of the king showed their resentment because they had to toil hard during the sacrifice.

We can say that the people in early India followed all four methods of resistance against evil. They offered non-violent struggle and Magha did not resist grambhojaka but carried out constructive activities.

Thus, in the post-Christian era the size of kingdom increased and population became more heterogeneous but normally the people did not tolerate despots. The Jatakas the Arthashastra and the Mahabharata tell us that unjust king was killed by the people as they came to dethrone him. The Panchatantra also said that the enraged mob was a fearful thing.

References

Agrawala, V. S. (1968), *Bharat-Savitri* in three volumes, Sasta Sahitya, Delhi.

Bhagvat, D. (1980), *Siddhartha Jataka,* Vol. I, Varada, Pune.

Chousalkar, A. (1991), *The Theory of Rebellion in the Politics of Aristotle and Arthashastra of Kautilya*, Indological Book House, Delhi.

Kangle, R. P. (1969), *Prachin Bharatiya Rajniti,* Mauj Prakashan, Mumbai.

Kosambi, Dharmanand (2007), Buddhaleela, Maharashtra Sahitya and Sanskriti Mandal, Mumbai.

Kosambi, Dharmanand (2007), Jataka Katha Sangrah, Maharashtra Sahitya and Sanskriti Mandal, Mumbai.

More, S. (1995), *Krishna– His Life and Mission*, Gaaj Publications, Ahmednagar.

Pandey, U. C. (1979), *Political Concepts and Institutions in the Shukla Yajurveda*, Janaki, Patna.

Roychoudhuri, H. C. (1925), *Political History of Ancient India*, Calcutta University, Calcutta.

Saletore, B. A. (1971), Political ideas and Institutions in Ancient India, Bombay, Asia Publishing House.

Chapter – V

Revolts and Protests in Ancient India

In the present Chapter, we shall discuss revolts and forms of protest in the first millennium of the Christian era in ancient India. For this purpose, we have analysed the data available in two important books- the *Katha Sarit Sagar* and the *Rajatarangini*. Both the books were written in the twelfth century A.D. when the Hindu era was about to come to an end. These two texts presented the authentic information about the life of the people of that era. The *Katha Sarit Sagar* was written by a Kashmiri Pandit Somadeo and the *Rajatarangini* was also written by a Kashmiri historian Kalhan.

Introduction

The *Katha Sarit Sagar* or the ocean of stories was written by Somadeo. It was based on the great Prakrit work – '*Brihat Katha*' which was written by Gunadhya. He wrote the original work during the Satavahana period, perhaps in the first century A.D. Hence, we could see emergence of prosperity and growth of trade in these stories.

Gunadhya's Form of Protest

Gunadhya was a Brahmin pundit in the court of the Satavahana king. He was born in a Brahmin family and his mother and uncles died when he was young. He went to Southern India, learnt many sciences and came back to Pratishthan. He was appointed as a minister by the Satavahana king. The king wanted to learn Sanskrit within six months and Gunadhya said that he could not do so but one of the

Pandits said that he would do so. He did it successfully. Gunadhya did not accept his opponent's challenge to teach the king Sanskrit grammar within six months. As a result, he had to leave the court and use of Sanskrit language as well. He went to Vindhyachal along with a group of traders on the advice of a Bhilla tribal. While returning, he met, a tribe of the Pishachas and learnt their Paishachi language. It was different from Sanskrit but a variant of Prakrit languages. Gunadhya mastered the language and wrote his book '*Brihatkatha* in that language. He wrote seven books of stories. Each book was of one lakh verses and it took seven years for him to write the book. The total verses of the book were seven lakhs. Gunadhya decided to dedicate the '*Brihatkatha*' to the Satavahana king and his disciples went to the court of the king to do so. But the king said that this book was written in Paishachi language, hence, he did not value it. The book was returned. Gunadhya felt very unhappy and decided to burn down the book. He read out the story to animals and burnt that page in fire. He destroyed six books of that great work. When the king came to know about it, he came to jungle and requested Gunadhya not to burn the last book. He gave that book to the king and said that his disciples would explain it to him in Sanskrit language. The Satavahana king got the story translated in local languages. (Bhagavat, 2003: 1-110-112, 137-41)

Thus, Gunadhya followed the unique form of protest against the king. First, he wrote that great work in Paishachi when he was denied the right to use Sanskrit and secondly, he decided to burn when he was insulted by the king. Poets tend to do this even today. Now the '*Brihatkatha*' of Gunadhya in its original form is not available. Somadeva Sharma wrote his *Katha Sarit Sagar* – the ocean of stories based on the then available version of the *Brihatkatha*. Kashmiri Pandit Kshemendra also wrote a book the Brihat Katha Manjiri. Somadeo wrote this book for queen Suryavati of king Ananta of Kashmir. The Brihat Katha consisted of one lakh verses and Somdeo's version consists of less than 25000 veres. Poets regarded the *Brihatkatha* on par with the great epics of the Ramayana and the *Mahabharata*. (1.4.5) There were several books and plays written on the basis of the stories from the *Brihatkatha* of Gunadhya.

Somadeva wrote this book to entertain queen Suryavati of king Ananta in eleventh century A.D. Ananta had two sons- elder son Kalasha was wicked and younger son Harsha was talented, intelligent but cruel. It was a turbulent period in the history of Kashmir. Ananta abdicated throne in favour of Kalash but again he claimed the throne. In 1077, he abdicated it because of revolt of Kalash and committed suicide. Somdeo wrote this story in the turbulent period of history. (1.6-7)

Ideology of Somadeva

Ideologically, the author of the *Katha Sarit Sagar* was closer to the Buddhist and Jaina traditions though officially he owed allegiance to the *Shaiva* philosophy. He remained loyal to the Vedic religion. Though he wrote the book in eleventh century, the stories contained in the book reflected the socio-political conditions of the pre-Gupta period of Gunadhya.

In one of the stories, he discussed the conflict between a Buddhist father and a Brahmanical son. Ratnadatta was a son of a rich Vaishya trader Vitashadatta. He condemned Buddhist religion and said that the Buddhist monks ate food without performing any daily rituals. They gave shelter to the lower castes people in their *Samgha* and they were interested in food only. His father told him that he should not condemn the religion of Buddha because of misbehaviour of few monks. In fact, Buddhism stood for truth and it showed compassion to all the living beings. It taught people not to fight on trivial issues. It pointed out that there should be no caste conflict. It stood for mercy and compassion and advocated the cause of universal brotherhood. Other religions also gave the same message. (Bhagvat, II-64-65) The Buddhist influence could be seen in other stories of the book when seven *parmitas* were taught through the stories. In one of the stories, a sage was attacked and beaten by the thieves. The thieves were caught by the king's men and he had decided to execute them for this crime. When the sage came to know about it, he requested the king to release the thieves because they were not responsible for this crime. Their weapons and anger which they got because of their evil deeds in the last birth were responsible. It is due to ignorance that men committed the crimes. He warned the king that, if these thieves were executed, he would commit suicide. The king accepted the request and the thieves were released. This was the 'Shama Parmita' taught by Buddha. (4.83-84)

Suicide as the Form of Protest

In the story of Deobhuti, Brahmin Deobhuti and his wife were staying in their home. A donkey of washerman strayed into their garden. Brahmin drove donkey away beating and injuring his leg. Angered by this the washerman came and the beat Brahmin and his wife. As a result, pregnant wife of Brahmin suffered abortion. Brahmin went to the chief of the city and complained about this. The chief called both of them and gave the decision that the Brahmin should do the donkey's work by carrying clothes on his back till the donkey's leg was restored to health. Similarly, since the washerman's beating caused the abortion of the Brahmin's wife, it was his duty to make her pregnant! After listening to this strange sentence and judgment, the Brahmin and his wife decided to commit suicide and they took poison. When the king of the land came to know about this, he arrested and executed the chief of the city. (4.79-80).

Sacrifice of Vineet Mati

In this book, there is a famous story of Jimutvahana, who sacrificed his own life to save the life of innocent snake. (4.272-75) Harsha wrote a play 'Naganand' on the basis of this story only.

Another story in this tradition is that of king Vineet Mati who was a popular king. Vineet Mati had a friend called Indu-Kalash. He helped Indu Kalash to secure the throne by driving his brother Kanak Kalash out of his kingdom. Kanak Kalash thought that Vineet Mati had done injustice to him. Therefore, he threatened him that he would commit suicide in protest against injustice done to him. Vineet Mati realised that he had committed a mistake and to make amends to that, he offered his own kingdom to Kanak Kalasha. When the citizens and ministers came to know about it, they opposed the king. The citizens came out on the streets and protested against the decision of the king. They wanted the king not to resign. But Vineet Mati refused to change his decision. He renounced kingdom in favour of Suvarna Kalash and retired to jungle to perform penance. (IV, 76-77)

Brave Protest by Three Women

In the *Brihatkatha Shloka Sangraha* of Budhswami, there is a story of king Mahasena of Ujjayani. He had two sons – Gopala and Palaka. Gopala was named as king and Palaka as his crown Prince. But in order to acquire power immediately, Gopala killed his father Mahasena and became king. But the people did not like this unjust patricide. One day Gopala was moving about in the city mounting on the elephant. But suddenly, the elephant got wild and started killing people on his way. A girl was captured by the elephant in its trunk. But the girl managed to ride the back of the elephant and fearlessly told the king, "Person who had no compunction in killing his own father would kill ordinary people also. There is no surprise in this." The king moved ahead. A prostitute stopped and admonished him for killing his own father. Later on he was also harshly criticised by a Brahmin woman. Deeply hurt by these admonitions, Gopala decided to renounce the kingship in favour of his brother Palaka and retired to jungle. (Vol. I, Int. 10-11)

Another important aspect of the *Katha Sarit Sagar* is existence of a large number of tribal kings. They belonged to Bhilla, Pulinda, Shabar and Kirat communities. They had their own kingdoms and armies. They supported revolts. Some of them gave shelters to robbers.

In the stories of the book, we have several examples of their participation in protest.

Punishment for Treason

The king of Varanasi was betrayed by his three Brahmin colleagues who hatched a conspiracy to kill him but he survived the assassination attempt. His name was Putrak. He retired in jungle and his old friends went to Varanasi to capture political power but when the ministers of the king came to know about it they killed them for treason. (Vol. I, 89-82)

In the first volume of the K'Sagar, there is a story of Chanakya who vowed to destroy Nanda king for insulting him and he succeeded in it. He did it with the help of Chandragupta. (Vol. I, 108-9)

Sacrifice of Jimuta Vahana

Jimuta Vahana in his earlier life, was plundered by thieves. They wanted to sacrifice him but he was saved by a Bhill a king, who became his friend. His friendship with a Bhill king was admired by citizens. There was young Naga-Shankhchuda who was to be eaten by Garuda due to his turn to sacrifice himself according to the agreement reached between Garuda and the Nagas. Jimuta Vahana volunteered to go instead of Shankhachuda. Due to his sacrifice, the heart of Garuda got transformed. He thought that out of anger, he had killed many Nagas, hence, he wanted to commit suicide in repentence. Jimuta Vahana told him "If you have really resolved not to commit sin, you expiate all your past sins. You stop killing the beings. Expiation and resolve to follow the path of non-killing was enough, there is no need of committing suicide." (Vol. I, 337-40) The same story was repeated in Vol. 4 of the book with some variation. In this story, Jimut Vahana criticised king of Nagas Vasuki for sacrificing his own people to save his own skin. He said that Vasuki should have enlisted his own name first for the sacrifice. Shankhachuda in this story, ran after Jimut Vahana and pleaded with Garuda to kill him instead of Jimut Vahana. After seeing the resolve of both of them of self-sacrifice, Garuda decided to stop the killings. Here Shankhachuda called Jimut Vahana an incarnation of Bodhisattva. (Vol. 4, 261-74)

Somdatta was a son of Brahmin Agni-Datta who was an insolent fool. His younger brother was moderate and learned. Somdatta committed violence against an elderly Brahmin. After his complaint, king sent in his servant to fetch him. But he was killed by Somdatta. He was arrested and the king sentenced him to death, but due to the request of his brother, it was commuted. He wanted to leave the kingdom along with his relatives. (I-292-93)

Victory of Truth

There is a story of victory of truth over the evil. In the kingdom of Ujjayani, there was a minister called Nagarjuna who had the characteristics of Bodhisattva. He was not liked by the Queen. Hence, she asked the king to demand the head of Nagarjuna. He willingly gave it. It was a supreme sacrifice. The king of the state–Chirayu did not like this and left the kingdom in anguish. Jivahara became the king. But sons of Nagarjuna didn't like this. They raised a banner of revolt against the king and in the ensuing battles Jivahara was killed. His mother died due to the shock of death of her son. One of the sons of the king Chirayu, Shatayu became the king. He was anointed by the ministers of the state. (Vol. II, 272-76)

Sometimes, the ministers led the forces against the oppressive kings. There is a story of minister Gunasharma of Ujjayini. King Mahasena suspected that he had dishonoured his queen. He wanted to punish him in the Court of the king but Gunasharma escaped. He organised his forces, attacked Ujjayini and told the people the evil deeds of the king and the queen. He defeated and drove out Mahasena and himself became the king. (Vol. II, 410-17)

Mistake Amended

Sometimes, the king made mistakes in pronouncing sentences and the good people intervened to tell him the truth. There was a trader named Samudra Datta. He was married to Vasudatta. Once Samudra Datta came to father-in-law's house. That day his wife went to meet her paramour at night. But considering him as a thief, he was caught and executed by the police! A thief who came to steal at her father's house, followed her out of curiosity. Vasudatta came back and accused her husband of the crime. The king ordered that Samudra Gupta should be executed for the crime. He was taken for the execution but the thief who was a witness to the event realised that an innocent man was being punished, hence he told truth to the king's officers. The king realised the mistake, released the trader and made the thief the Sheriff of the city. (IV, 179-80)

Forms of Protest in the Katha Sarit Sagar

The *Katha sarit sagar* was written by Somdatta when Kashmir was undergoing turbulent part of its history and there was a lot of violence, and cruelty in the society. Somdeo narrated the stories of Gunadhya in such a manner that the reader would grasp importance of love, compassion and justice. He narrated noble lives of the people who sacrificed, kingdom and household to uphold the cause of truth.

Thus, in the *Katha Sarit Sagar*, there are a number of stories that describe the forms of protest the people used against the oppressive king or against the wrong decisions of the government. In some cases, the people revolted, killed the king and elected new king. Sometimes, they migrated to other state. Sometimes, they committed suicide. Jimutvahana followed the Buddhist ethics and preached the gospel of self-sacrifice to effect the change of heart. Such a change of heart was effected when Garuda decided to stop the massacre of innocent Nagas. There is a strong moral bias in the stories of the *Katha Sarit Sagar.* One can see continuity between the *Jataka* stories and stories in the *Katha Sarit Sagar* because the people normally followed same methods that were followed in the *Jatakas*. The brigandage continued to remain the method of political resistance and in both the books, the tribal kings provided protection to them. The relationship between capital city, rural areas and the frontier areas was not always harmonious. The people selected their own king when there was vacancy. The bedecked royal elephant garlanded the worthy person and the people selected him as the king. Due to this procedure, which was completely impersonal, the royal authority was accepted by the people.

The people were hostile to the wicked king and they thought that the evil king was some sort of ghoul who struck terror in the minds of the people. They took recourse to following forms of protest to highlight the cases of injustice and to correct the wrong course of action.

(1) When the kings pronounced harsh sentence to the innocent persons or even to their near and dear, without making proper inquiry, the people protested and tried to tell the king that a particular person was not guilty. Sometimes, the condemned person was released from the gallows.

(2) The people got themselves organised and killed wicked king. It was a mass action of the furious mob. The *Panchatantra* had said that the enraged populace was a fearsome thing. Sometimes, the leadership was provided by prominent people.

(3) The hapless couple like Devahuti and his wife were condemned to such a decision that they had committed suicide in protest because they saw no way out of the situation. Sometimes the victims threatened to commit suicide and got their grievances redressed. Due to this, sometimes the kings changed their decisions and sometimes they did not. If they continued to do injustice, their moral authority was adversally affected.

(4) Jimut Vahana effected change of heart of cruel Garuda who continued to wreak vengeance against the Nagas because of cheating, slavery and insults imposed on his mother. Jimut Vahana freed him from the cycle of revenge and vendetta.

(5) The revolts of the people were supported by the frontier tribal chiefs or the kings of the neighbouring states, according to their own interests. Sometimes they captured the kingdom.

Kalhana and Rajatarangini

The '*Rajatarangini*' of Kalhana was another important book which was written during the same period. Both Somadeva and Kalhana belonged to Kashmir. Somadeva wrote his book during the reign of king Ananta of Kashmir and Kalhana wrote after 50 years in the reign of Jaisinha. It was roughly twelfth century A.D. Both the books showed the decline of Hindu civilisation though they did not think that the Muslims would eventually take over most of north India within next 100 years. Kalhana was a son of a minister of a Kashmir king and he had written this historical work to tell the story of the kings of Kashmir upto twelfth century A.D. He described the history of Kashmir in eight Chapters. As a historian, he maintained strict neutrality and wrote, "That man of merit alone deserves praise whose language like that of a judge in recounting the events of the past has discarded the bias as well as prejudice." (Kalhana, 2004: 1-7)

The *Rajatarangini* was translated by Mr. Ranjit Pandit in English Pandit Nehru has written an erudite 'Foreword' to the book. While admiring Kalhan's ability to tell the authentic history of Kashmiri people, he wrote, "We read of Suyya's great engineering feets and irrigation works; of Lalitaditya's distant wars of conquest in far off countries; of Meghavahana's curious attempt to spread non-violence by conquest; of building of temples and monasteries and their destruction by unbelievers and the iconoclasts who confiscated the temple treasures. And then there were famines, floods and great fires which decimated the population and reduced survivors to misery." (X) He further pointed out: "Popular risings take place and Kalhana describes Kashmir as a country which delighted in insurrection and they are exploited by military leaders and adventurers to their advantage. We reach the end of that period of decay which ultimately ushered in the Muslim conquest of India." (XI) The book was translated in many languages has 8 chapters and 786 verses. It is written in Vaidarbhi style. (Singh, 1970: 4)

Salient Features of the RajaTarangini

Ranjit Pandit wrote an introductory note 'Invitation' to describe the salient features of the great work. He held that this work was composed in 1151 A.D. by Kalhana who was a son of a minister. Singh held that he took two years to complete the work. (4) He had free access to the royal court seconds but he didn't write eulogical accounts of the kings. He maintained strict neutrally while describing the doings of the kings, Brahmins, Dombs, Chandalas and princes without any prejudice. According to Pandit, Kalhana was by nature philosophical and he saw in every crisis, the clash between the good and the evil. (XX) He was liberal in his approach and though he was born in the family of a minister, he displayed a great concern for poor people. He was influenced by philosophies of Buddha and Mahaveer. Hence Pandit wrote, "Due to warmth and generosity of his heart, Kalhana's heart goes out to the poor, and the downtrodden; he reveals his sympathy for the underdog, denounces forced labour and expresses his horror of the slave trade of the *Mlechchas*." (XXX) History to him was not something to learn but something to make people live and understand life. He gives both sides of all questions and points out the faults and the virtues of the actors. His observations show that the achievements of the great were merely the answers to the big needs of the society and the success was only possible because the time was ripe". (XXXI)

Dharmanand Kosambi's Interpretation

During Kalhana's time, feudalism was completely established in Kashmir and in the Kashmir society. Brahmins played a key role, not as priests but as ministers, generals and officers. A Brahmin foot soldier Rokka became Prime Minister because of his abilities. There was relative absence of ideological controversies in Kashmir. The kings were often coming from doubtful lineages. Uppal was a founder of the empire and he was a son of spirit distiller. The Karkota dynasty was of still lower tribal origin. Tunga who was the virtual ruler of Kashmir in eleventh century, came from so called the lowest caste. *Agraharas* given to Brahmins was a sort of private property. The class of Damaras which meant local chief with some military power played key role in the politics. The quarrel between the Damaras and the kings became the principal motif of Kashmirian history (Kosambi, 1985: 121). They made and unmade kings, fought battles with the central power as well as among themselves. They occupied the most cultivated part of Kashmir. According to Dr. Kosambi the society depicted in the book was a feudal society which was interested in increase in the commodity production by local concentration of surplus by the use of force in the hands of nobles. (126)

There was considerable influence of the Buddhist ethics on Kalhana and he said : "the Bodhisattvas had conquered sorrow against every wrong doer, they do not grow anger, but through forgiveness return good for evil,. They who desire enlightenment not for self alone are bent on the salvation of the world." (RT 1-138-139) After listening to this, the king changed his policy of the persecution of the Buddhists and constructed the Viharas. Thus, Kalhana understood the ethical aspects of Buddhist philosophy though he himself was a *Shaiva*.

Unjust King Punished

Kalhana narrated a story of a king who developed attraction for a

Brahmin's wife who was a daughter of a Naga chief. He tried to seduce her but she refused. The evil king sent his soldiers to secure and to bring her to his palace. She took shelter in the house of a Naga chief who was her father. The chief attacked the king and burnt him as well as his city. In the process, he killed a large number of people. But he had to leave the palace in remorse because the ordinary people denounced him for the slaughter he committed. Kalhana wrote: 'under the guise of protecting the subjects such a type of destroyers emerge of a sudden, now and then and cause destruction." (1-269) Thus, Kalhana did not favour killings of innocent people. It was his opinion that due to good actions in the past of the subjects, the kings appeared to rescue a kingdom deep sunk in disaster. Those who intended to follow the policy of harassment of subjects, perished along with their families. On the other hand the fortune waited on the lineal descendants of those who reinstated order where there was chaos. (1.187-88)

He graphically described the aggression and killings of the people by the Huna king Mihirkula and criticised the Brahmins for accepting gifts from such a cruel king. (1.307) about Mihirkula he said : "Thus, although the wicked that the king had not been assassinated by the people in the uprising, he was protected by the very gods who had urged him to do that act." (1.324) He informed that owing to the dawn of superior merit of subjects' good actions, the king at last perished, his son Baka the righteous was crowned as the king by subjects. (1.325)

Revolt Against the Inefficient King

Then he described the revolt of the people against king Yudhishthira who did not govern his state righteously. Due to wrong advise of the ministers, the state administration was in disarray and there was disorder. As a result, the ministers of the king organised people and encircled the palace of the king. The king pleaded for reconciliation but they refused his terms of reconciliation. He wrote : "Then having formed a league, they surrounded with armed forces the royal palace, drowning the shouts of men with the terrible rattle of the kettle drums, they obstructed the light of the sun by the shadows of their standards borne by an array of an intoxicated elephant which darkened even by the day, terraces palace." After the battle, the king requested the safe passage from the kingdom and left Srinagar along with his wives" (1.366-67). Thus, the king was exiled to Himalaya and Vikramaditya was chosen as the king.

During this period, Kashmir was visited by terrible famine in which a large number of the people perished. King Tunjina tried to help people with compassion and strove hard to overcome the distress of the people. He was moved by great anguish and thought that the subjects were suffering hunger and still he hadn't been in a position to offer support to them. It was wrong on his part to live like this. Hence, he decided to commit suicide in frustration as he was not in a position to see of end destruction of his subjects. (2.41) But his wife told him that this was not the right course of action and advised him to exert hard to protect his subjects. (2.45-49) The king strove hard and helped his subjects overcome famine.

Sandhimata was Winner

Kalhana narrated a story of king Jayendra who became jealous of his wise Minister Sandhimata and banished him from the court and lodged him in the prison. After the lapse of 10 years, the wicked king decided to impale him in prison at the hands of his cruel officers. Through the good offices of his teacher- Ishan, Sandhimati escaped. He ran away and grouped his forces and encircled the city. The people elected Sandhimati as the king of Kashmir. He administered the kingdom righteously (2.114-18) But due to his inability to govern the state property the people were disaffected and the state faction riddle. In due course decided to leave kingship. Kalhana wrote, "he convened a meeting of the subjects and in the midst of conference, delivered the good government to them like a fixed deposit which had been safely guarded." (2-159) The subjects followed him in anguish and gave him farewell.

Militant Non-Violence of King Megha Vahana

After Sandhimata, the Ministers went to Gandhara to bring Megha Vahana as the king. Meghavahana endeared himself to the people because of his righteous policies. Kalhana wrote: "Even the lives of Bodhisattvas who were compassionate towards living beings, the large-hearted king excelled by his noble conduct." (3-4) He declared his policy of non-slaughter of animals throughout the kingdom. He asked the people to offer the animal effigy of the butter instead of animal in the sacrifices. He built great Viharas. One day, there was a shout against the thieves. The king asked two servants to arrest them. They were arrested and produced before the king. Meanwhile, their owner came requesting clemency from the king. He released them asking them to follow the path of Dharma. In order to compel the rulers to desist from violence to living beings, he launched a campaign of conquest. He defeated a large number of kings in war and made them follow the path of non-violence! A Shabara tribal wanted to sacrifice a person to bring his son back to sound health. The king wanted to save the victim as well as the son of the Shabara. Hence, he offered his own body for sacrifice- so that both of them could live. (3.29-30) He told him, "The wishing tree and the dharma couldn't be compared, since the former yields fruits upon being requested, the latter do so of its own accord." (3.64) Meghavahana went upto Lanka to teach the gospel of non-violence. (3.74-75) As a result, the king Matrigupta ordered the prohibition of animal slaughter in his kingdom.

The King and the Right of the Leather Worker

Chandrapida was a good king who followed the righteous policy. He wanted to construct the temple of Tribhuvan Swami on a particular piece of land. The land belonged to a leather worker who refused to give his land and a hut in which he lived. The officers of the king offered him money and other gifts but he did not relent. He came and complained to the king. The king criticised his officers for confiscating the land without taking the owner's permission. He told his officers, "Stop the construction or build it somewhere else, by seizing the land of others, who would tarnish an act of piety!" (4.58-59) He did not want to impose unlawful procedure. He said "it was ourselves, who are judges of what is right and unright enforce procedure which is unlawful who should tread the path of law? The leather worker came to meet him and said that there was a conflict between the king and an ordinary person and as a judge he expected impartial behaviour from the king. He said, "I am not less than a dog and the king is not greater than Ramchandra, why do then the Councillors get agitated as it were at their private task between you and me?" He told the king that he was proud of his own body as the king was proud of his bedecked body. He was as proud of his small hut which had a mouth of earthen pot as its window, which brought cool wind to him, as the king was proud of his palaces! This small cottage, like his mother was witness to both his happy and unhappy moments in life. He could not bear to see it leveled to the ground. (4.66-71) He further said; "the distress of mankind at the seizer of their dwelling house either an immortal falling from 'Vimana' or a king deposed from sovereignty is capable of describing it. Notwithstanding this, if after coming to my dwelling place, your majesty were to ask for it, yielding to the rule of good manners, it would be proper thing for me to give it." (4.67-73)

Chandrapida understood the import of the speech and personally went to his hut. He requested him to give his land for the construction of temple and promised suitable compensation to the leather worker. The wise worker praised the king for his righteousness and said, "Oh! king! yielding to another under the compelling influence of the law is proper on your part. As in the past, that of Pandu's son by Dharma in the form of a dog so by me who an untouchable has been tested to-day the righteousness in your case." (4.75-76)

Protest Fast by Brahmin Woman

A Brahmin woman went on a protest fast due to untimely death of her husband, who had no enemy. It was believed in ancient India that man faced untimely death because of imperfection of the king. The woman blamed a Brahmin for using sorcery to kill her husband. She threatened to end her life by fasting if a murderer of her husband was not punished. King Chandrapida was in great anguish. He himself went on three days' fast. While fasting, he received the divine instructions. On the basis of these instructions, he arrested the guilty Brahmin and tested and punished him. The woman admired the king for punishing the guilty of secret crime. (4.93-17)

Chandrapida's brother Tarapida was of evil nature and he used the services of the same enraged Brahmin to use witchcraft to end the life of Chandrapida. (4.112) Earlier the wicked Brahmin was not executed by Chandrapida because he thought that he had acted at someone's behalf. Chandrapida lost throne and Tarapida became king, he was a wicked king and he oppressed the people. He decided to punish Brahmins and meted out severe punishments to them. There was a rising tide of anger against him. Ultimately, he was made to wear out by Brahmins by using the methods of witchcraft. Hence, Kalhana concluded, "He who in order to injure others devises a plan through that very one he is, forsooth, ruined, fire gives birth to smoke which blinds the eye after becoming it extinguishes that very fire by the torrents of water." (4.125)

Lalitaditya- A Great Conqueror

Tarapida's rule was followed by that of great conqueror Lalitaditya who was one of the greatest conquerors in Indian history. He made conquests all over India and constructed beautiful temples. He issued following instructions to his ministers as far as the policy of the state was concerned:

(1) There should be no dissension among the leading elements of the country because it is more dangerous than the invasion of enemy.

(2) The dwellers in the mountainous regions should be fined even though they had committed no crime because should they accumulate wealth, they could build fortifications, take shelter in them and become treasonable.

(3) The people living in the villages should not be allowed to accumulate foodgrains excess of their annual consumption. If they were allowed to have excessive wealth, they could become terrible Damaras in a single year and were able to violate the authority of the king. He further maintained "when once the rural population secures railments, women, woollen blankets, food, drinks, horses, dwellings which are the worthy of the capital, when the fortifications which ought to be cared for are neglected, through the arrogance by the kings, when they show lack of appreciation of

> charters of their officers, when from a single district is exacted maintenance of the army, when the civil servants had formed a league of matrimonial alliances with one anothers, when the kings take the same view as the civil servants of the state; then it may be known without doubt that there have been a reversal of good of the subjects." (4.349-52)

This was the advise of the great emperor to his ministers.

Subaltern Defence of the King

Great conqueror Lalitaditya was succeeded by his son Kuvalayapida who was a supporter of peace. Initially, he was perturbed by the disobedience of his authority by ministers. He decided to abdicate the throne in favour of comfort of quietism and in order to achieve inner peace. (4.389-90)

After succession of three kings, Jayapida became the king. He marched far away on conquest of distant lands, his wife's brother named Jajja captured the power and became the king. Jayapida suffered because many of his followers defected. But Jajja's rule was not liked by the citizens. They wanted to bring back king Jayapida. When Jayapida came to punish Jajja, a large number of villagers and woodsmen came to support the king. Srideva- a village Chandala assumed the leadership and went in for Jajja. He saw thirsty Jajja drinking water mounting on the horse. He used sling to hit a stone on his face which killed Jajja instantly. (4.975-77) Thus, Jayapida's throne was saved by the sabaltarn elements.

Brahmin Revolt Against Excessive Taxes

Jayapida levied excessive taxes on the people and punished those who did not pay them. He committed many atrocities on the people. He and his officers became more covetous. The Brahmins of Kashmir decided to show courage and challenged the might of the king by undertaking fast unto death. They started killing themselves by jumping in fire. The king didn't care and continued his policy of repression. 99 Brahmins embraced death in protest. The king made amendment in his policy and decided not to confiscate the property of the Brahmins but he continued the policy of repression, Brahmins didn't relent. They came and told the king that he was pursuing unjust policy and due to Brahmin outrage, he could suffer the same punishment as other kings in the past suffered. The king laughed and challenged them to curse and kill him. He pooh-poohed them for these tall claims. Kalhana informed us that suddenly a golden pole dropped from the canopy on the person of the king and he got severely injured. After some days, he died because of injury. (4.619-57) Jayapida was brought back to power by the people but due to his repressive policy, he forced Brahmins to launch fast unto death against the repressive policy.

Unjust Kings Assassinated

The successor of Jayapida, Lalitapida was wicked and his government followed repressive policy. He became covetous and started persecution of his subjects. The king's son Gopal Varman was a sensible person. Hence, he asked his father to change his policy which had ruined the lives of the subjects and he had become unpopular. He requested the king to abolish king's tax, which was originated in greed. The king did not accept the request and passed unpleasant remarks. He said, "You yourself this day grant one boon to me that, when you have secured sovereign power, you willn't oppress the subjects more than this!" (5.202) The king faced problems. His 20 sons died without any ailment facing the curse of subjects. The king went on expedition, punishing the rebellious chiefs. During that period, he was killed by an arrow discharged by a Svapaka posted on the hill it pierced his neck unaware and he died. (5.218) He was succeeded by his son Gopal Varman who was a man of piety and good behaviour. His mother Sugandha developed love affairs with one Prabhakar. He became powerful. He was made the treasurer and amassed a lot of wealth. He defeated the Shahi rulers of Punjab. Gopal Varman did not like rising power of Prabhakar but he was ineffective. Ramdeva, an employee of Prabhakar killed Gopal Varman by burning him to death. (5.240) Shankar Varman was made the king but he died within ten days. The king Chakra Varman took the office. He grew arrogant and committed many crimes. He was killed by the Damaras (armed group of people) in order to take revenge of killing of the Damaras. (5.409)-11) It is the argument of Kalhan that due to the sins of subjects only the sinful kings assumed power. (5.415)

Wicked King Dies

Wicked king Unmattamati killed his two brothers as well as his father Partha to capture power. His wickedness knew no bounds as he ripped open abdomen of women to see foetus as an endurance test of the bodies. He killed ordinary workers. But some Brahmins accepted *agraharas* from such an evil king. He died because of T.B. and everybody including his queens rejoiced at his death. (5.440-45) There was no successor to this king.

Election of the New King

There was no king. Hence, the Brahmin Pandits were asked by the ministers to elect the king, and for almost four or five days, they were not in a position to appoint any one as the king. The Chief of the army Kamal Vardhan expected the nomination but the Brahmins refused to do so and they unanimously decided to nominate Yashaskara as the king. He was coroneted and assumed the charge as the king. He was a learned man but was wandering like a destitute. He received the kingship because of providence. (5.477-78)

After assuming office, he decided to keep a distance from Brahmins and told them that they should not come to the palace without any business. He respected them but they shouldn't be elated with pride that they had elected him as the king. He was a good ruler. He made the land free of robbers and the high roads became safe for travellers.

Hunger Strike of a Brahmin

During his regime, a Brahmin began hunger strike because he was deceived by a merchant and the dishonest officers of the king supported the fraudulent merchant. He was called for discussion. He said that due to poverty, he could not pay back the debt to the merchant and he settled the matter with him by selling his land. There was a well in the land which was not sold by the Brahmin because he left it for his wife as a source of livelihood. But the merchant did not give the well to the wife of the Brahmin who had gone out to earn livelihood. Because of this, the wife had to work as a maid servant. After coming back, he lodged a case against the merchant in the court. But most of the judges gave judgment in favour of the merchant. Hence, in order to demand justice, he sat on hunger strike. The king summoned the fresh court and asked the judges to explain their position. They said that the well was sold along with the land and the Brahmin was a cheat. But the king decided to personally investigate the case. He found that the Brahmin was right and the merchant was a cheat. The king ordered to restore property to the Brahmin and expelled the merchant from the kingdom. (5.17-43) He also restored 100 gold coins to a Brahmin who was deprived of the same by a villager. But Kalhana said that Yashaskara became greedy, covetous and debauch and as a result, despite his good work, he became unpopular. His health was not sound hence, he decided to leave the throne, for his son Sangramadeva. But his minister Parshvagupta assassinated Sangramadeva in his own palace and captured power. (6.126-29)

Brahmins and Hunger Strikes

Parshvagupta's son Kshemagupta was of a wicked nature. An evil Queen Didda became the master and killed many people. Her paramour Tunga became the most important person. He was a good military leader. Didda's brother Vigraharaja incited Brahmins to launch hunger strike against Tunga and the queen. The Brahmins formed a group, and started fast unto death. The people who were against Tunga wanted to kill him. But Didda entered into the dialogue with the Brahmins. She persuaded and bribed them and as a result, they withdrew their fast. After sometime, Vigrahasena again incited Brahmins to undertake hunger strike. Since Brahmins wanted more bribe, they began hunger strike. Tunga decided to punish Brahmins. He attacked them and drove them out of the city. (6.335-45) He arrested those Brahmins who took bribe and put them in prison. (6.347) Thus, Tunga proved that the fasts were politically motivated.

The fight between Tunga and Brahmins continued but Tunga was a match to their Machiavellian mechanisms. Some Brahmin ministers incited Brahmins to start hunger strike. They demanded resignation of king. They were ready to lower their demand if Tunga was expelled from the kingdom. But they started putting more demands. Meanwhile during the fast a Brahmin died and the Brahmins refused to cremate body of the Brahmin and held Tunga responsible for his death. They brought somebody else's body for cremation! They were incited by politicians and as a result, the fight broke out between supporters and opponents of Tunga. Tunga defeated and imprisoned them. Brahmins ran away out of fear. (7.10-26) Tunga was killed in the battle that was fought, with the invading army of Mohamad Gazani. As a result the struggle between Brahmins and Tunga was over.

Ananta, Kalasha and Harsha

There was a conflict between king Ananta and his son Kalasha. Ananta abdicated his throne in favour of Kalasha because of intervention of the queen. At that time, Brahmins decided to undertake hunger strike to bring about reconciliation between the father and the son as their conflict ruined the country. Both the father and the son agreed and peace was restored. (7.400-401) But peace was temporary. Ananta gave kingship to Kalasha but he was a wicked king. He got kingship because of his mother. But real power remained with Ananta. Kalasha was not popular.

Harsha was second the son of king and he was a good poet, dancer, singer and extremely intelligent person. His songs were sung by the people and because of that he was popular. He was instigated by his close supporters to assassinate the king. But he could not do so. The king was in great agony. Ananta ordered Harsha to be imprisoned. Harsha undertook fast in jail because he feared that he would be poisoned. His father died and the ministers appointed his younger brother Utkarsha as the king. Harsha went on fast for release from the prison. Harsha managed to overthrow the regime of Utkarsha. Being cornered by the enemy forces, king Utkarsha committed suicide by stabbing himself to death. Citizens welcomed Harsha. (7.846-60) Harsha was the most cruel and repressive king the state had ever seen. Kalhana had pointed out extreme contradictions in his personality. (7.869-73)

Harsha suppressed many revolts against him with heavy hand. Initially, he was popular among the masses but he became extremely cruel and executed most of the young princes of the family including sons of his brother. He grew covetous and decided to plunder the temples in Kashmir. He destroyed all the images of gods barring two in order to get gold out of than. He appointed a minister for that purpose.

Brahmins raised their voice against this and they began hunger strike against the king. At that time, the Harsha paid compensation to them. (7.1088) Images were destroyed, they were despoiled and thrown in the dung. Kalhana wrote : "that only two gods survived Harsha's war against images. He imposed new taxes on the people." But despite all his crimes, covetousness, immorality, he didn't face the revolts of the people as he ruled the state firmly though Damaras continued to revolt against him. But he defeated them. (87.1328) But he was attacked by two brothers-Ucchala and Sussala. His armies suffered defeats. His own son Bhoja was killed in the battle. He lost his kingdom. Ultimately, he was encircled and killed by the soldiers of Ucchala. Ucchala succeeded Harsha and compared to Harsha, he was a righteous king, and carried out a number of welfare activities. During this period Brahmins started hunger strike against general Sujjain. (8-2076)

Violent Satyagraha of Vijayraj

There was a wicked minister of king and his name was Chitraratha. He imposed heavy taxes on the people and followed extremely repressive policies. Brahmins decided to oppose it and at Avantipura, they began hunger strike. Many Brahmins made supreme sacrifice by jumping in the blazing fire. When a cowherd saw this, out of the grief he also burnt himself to death. (8.2224-26) This created revulsion in the minds of the people. But wicked minister did not mend his ways. The king also supported him. There was a young man called Vijayraj who was agitated because of loss of lives of number of Brahmins. He thought there was no alternative but to kill the wicked minister.

He has discussion with his brother. He told his brother that it was no good to take life of man and non-violence was the highest form of dharma but in this situation he would have to take recourse to violence. Even great people occasionally took to violence to end the mischief. He thought that he should assassinate evil minded Chitraratha to save the lives of fasting Brahmins. He decided to kill him. He relentlessly pursued Chitraratha attacked and struck him. He was taken to the interior. The king consoled the minister and asked him who attacked him? Vijayraj disclosed his identity and said that he had killed the minister. When the soldiers of the king tried to catch him, he fought heroically and injured 20 soldiers in the battle. He perished in the struggle. (8.2250-54)

Vijayraj gave three reasons for the killing of minister:

(1) The king was supporting the wicked minister and the conditions of the people needed to be improved by removing the minister from the scene.

(2) By sacrificing his own body, he could save lives of many and make lives of endless people happy.

(3) It was right to kill unrighteous person for the universal benefit, even the Jina slew the dragon to put an end the threat to living human beings. (8.2229-36)

Vijayraj suffered injuries and died.

Soldiers found in his arm a little note on which the motive of the act was described. It read, "To safeguard the righteous for the destruction of evil doers and with a view to reinstate the sacred law, I come to life in each age." Kalhana wrote : "His affirmation, at the last moment, in virtue of this verse, sanctified him." (8.2256-57) Needless to say that this was the famous verse from the Bhagavat Geeta which Lord Krishna pronounced. Thus, we could call him first violent Satyagrahi who embraced death in the cause of justice. He could have very easily escaped after attacking Chitraratha but he stood the ground and faced the death like a true warrior.

Forms of Protest

Kalhana in the 'Rajatarangini' gave a lot of information about the forms of protest used by the people against the oppressive rulers. Following were important forms of protest followed by the people:

(1) The people came on the street and complained to the king about injustice done to them by the officers of the king. Many times, kings took corrective steps.

(2) The unjust and oppressive kings faced revolts from the people and even cruel kings like Harsha suffered defeat and death. Revolts got the support of the people and other powerful sections of the society because due to unrighteous policies of the king, he had lost his authority to rule.

(3) Hunger strike by an individual was also a form of protest in which many times, the agitator got justice.

(4) Hunger strikes was the special weapon used by the people against the king. Kings appointed officers to watch the cases of hunger strikes (Pandit, 2004: 723) The hunger strikes were normally led by Brahmins who sacrificed their bodies when the oppressive policies of the king did not end. Therefore, hunger strike was an important weapon in the hands of the people.

(5) Many a times, hunger strikes were started at the behest of a minister who wanted to settle score with other officer. Therefore, there were professional fast-mongers who were incited by the political players. These fasts were withdrawn, when there was reconciliation between the two. Sometimes, a tough political player like Tunga used methods of bribery and force to break the politically motivated hunger strikes. Kalhana informed us that these Brahmins undertook hunger strike to get more bribe. But all fasts were not like this.

(6) Sometimes Brahmins went on fast to force two opposing parties to reconcile their differences as their mutual warfare was causing hardships to the people and killing a large number of people. They forced king Ananta and his son to have reconciliation which resulted in temporarily Ananta leaving the throne.

(7) Even an ordinary person stood tall against the king when it came to safeguarding his rights and his honour. The leather worker told the mighty king that his small hut was as valuable to him as many palaces of the king. He could give him the land and the hut, if a proper request was personally made by the king. He protested still his honour was respected by the king.

(8) Kalhana like other Indian thinkers believed that the unrighteous kings were punished by God, if they escaped the punishment by people. Many evil kings lost their lives because they suffered incurable diseases. Jayapida was the most wicked king who imposed heavy taxes and when 99 Brahmins committed suicides he laughed and asked protesting Brahmins to curse him. Kalhana informed us that he was killed in an accident. This was a divine intervention. Kalhana believed that though at times, righteousness might suffer, but ultimately the cause of dharma triumphed.

(9) Kalhana believed that the principle of self-sacrifice remained as the spring of action. The Bodhisattvas did not get angry because of wrong doings of others. They returned good for evil through the policy of forgiveness. They did not desire enlightenment for self alone but they wanted to achieve salvation for entire world. Vijayraj also believed in the principles of righteousness and universal beneficence and he thought that this could be achieved by self-sacrifice. He used force to end injustice because it was his contention that this was necessary to save the endless lives that could have been taken by the wicked Minister. He thought that it was his bounden duty to perform the task of reinstating Dharma in the world and freeing the world of evil doers in the interest of the good. He thought that this was his divine mission as the lord took birth in every age to save dharma.

(10) Due to opposition of the people and the hunger strikes undertaken by the Brahmins, several kings had to abandon their kingdoms and to seek exile in the jungles. Some of them perished in the jungles.

(11) The revolts in Kashmir were led by the crown princes, chiefs of the armed groups and powerful ministers of the kings. There was uneasy relations between the king and the Damaras who always challenged the might of the kings. Kings also tried to punish the Damaras when they were cornered. The reason for this conflict was the failure of the system to resolve contradiction of sharing of the surplus among the ruling classes.

(12) Meghavahana was a righteous king who tried to enforce non-violence in the country and for that purpose, he was ready to undertake the wars of conquest. He succeeded in spreading the message of non-violence.

Authors of the *Katha sarit sagar* and *Rajatarangini* are from Kashmir and they wrote their books in twelfth century A. D. In both the texts the people came out openly against injustice and there were a number of bad kings and ministers who tried to offend the people. They point out that if the unjust king was not brought down by the popular agitation, he would be punished by the divine intervention.

In Kashmir, there were pacifist kings like Meghavahana and most brilliant but the most oppressive kings like Harsha and the people had to deal with them. The people did not keep quite when injustice was taking place. The Damaras, weapon wielding warriors sometimes took part in the agitations but the most important role was played by Brahmins who collectively went on fast unto death and staked their own life against the king. Many of them died in the process. Brahmins in Kashmir followed the methods of protest initiated by the Brahmins in the Ramayana. Sometimes lower classes and the tribals came out in support of the king and foiled the designs of seditious elements. The story of Vijayraj needs special mention as he decided to kill the wicked minister after considerable deliberation. He did not run away from the scene and bravely embraced death. He believed that by killing a tyrant he was protecting the cause of Dharma. Thus, the

Rajatarangini stands out as a rare text of history in ancient India.

(13) Kalhana talked about the use of witchcraft against kings by the disaffected people. These 'abhichara' practices were mentioned by the Atharva Veda as well as by the Arthashastra of Kautilya.

References

Bhagvant, D. (2003), *The Katha Sarit Sagar* in five volumes, Varada, Pune (Translation was made by Mr. H. V. Bhave).

Kosambi, D. D. (1985), *D. D. Kosambi on History and Society – Problems of Interpretation,* Department of History, University of Mumbai.

Pandit, R. (2004), *The Rajatarangini*, Sahitya Academy, New Delhi.

Kosambi, Dharmanand (2007), Buddhaleela, Maharashtra Sahitya and Sanskriti Mandal, Mumbai.

Raghunath, Singh (1970), Kalhanas Rajtarangini, Varanasi, Hindi Pracharak Sanstha.

Chapter – VI

Political Authority and Forms of Political Protest in Indian Tradition: A Critical Study

In the preceding chapters, we have studied the nature of political authority in ancient India as well as the forms of political protest that were used by the people to voice their opposition to the oppressive policies of the government. We have traced the development of the methods and the forms from the *Atharvaveda* to the *Rajatarangini* of Kalhana through the *Jatakas*, the *Mahabharata*, the Kautilya's *arthashastra* and the *Katha Sarit Sagar* of Somadeva. The Katha-Sarit Sagar was based on the *Brihatkatha* of Gunadhya. In the present chapter, we shall discuss following issues in some detail :

(1) Nature of constitution of authority in ancient India and the methods of legitimisation.

(2) Ideologies of confrontation and reconciliation.

(3) Various forms of political protest.

(4) Continuities and contemporary relevance of forms of protest.

In the present study, we have covered the history of ancient India from the Vedic period to the twelfth century A.D. before the establishment of Muslim rule in north India. Mohammad Ghori began the invasions in the last decade of twelfth century and the slaves established their dynasty in the first decade of thirteenth century.

It took the Turks and the Pathans another 100 years to bring north and peninsular India under their control. Their rule continued for 500 years. Some of these forms of protests continued during the Muslim rule also. There is a continuity in the long tradition of dissent and protest which 'the Oriental despotism' endured. The people developed fearlessness against the most oppressive dictators as we could see it in the history of Kashmir.

Constitution of Political Authority in Ancient India

There was a serious discussion on the nature and constitution of political authority in ancient India. Basic theories of formation of state and constitution of authority were developed during the phase of the Janapada state. During this period, the state assumed territorial form as well as developed political identity. The state depicted in the *Mahabharata* and the *Jataka* stories was essentially Janapada state which had assumed distinct identity and developed some of the seven constituent elements. Thus, it was a developing state which could afford to sustain seven elements of the state. In the *Katha Sarit Sagar* and the *Rajatarangini* also, the size of the state was moderate, it was not a big empire.

In ancient Indian political thought, the problem of constitution of political authority was seriously considered because it is evident from the question posed by Yudhishthira to Bhishma in the Shantiparva (12.59) that there was curiosity about the nature of political power. Also, there is a discussion on the nature of *Danda* which symbolised political power. There is a clear understanding that the exercise of political power required use of force to punish the wrong doer and it might involve employment of violence. Hence, there was a constant need to justify the use of violence or *danda.* In the *Mahabharata*, there is an attempt to glorify *Danda* by giving it divine sanction but it is constantly emphasised that *Danda* cannot be used in anger or in self-interest. The person who has developed self-control could only use the *danda* in a proper manner because the purpose of punishment was to establish peace and to bring about reconciliation.

During the Vedic period, political authority was constituted through the election of the king. But along with election, certain religious sanctions were added through the consecration ceremony of the king. The ceremony was designed to legitimise the authority of the king by investing in him divine power as well as divine blessings. The entire consecration ceremony was organised to enlist the support of the leading elements of the society by involving them in various rituals. The *Ratnavamshi* ceremony was a good example of this involvement. It is constantly emphasized by Dr. Anand Coomarswami that this authority was limited by the ability of the king to hold fast to the path of *dharma*. The king had to first establish 'Swaraj' in his soul so that he could establish it in his state. (Coomarswami, 1978: 82-83) In both the Vedic and the Buddhist traditions, legitimacy of royal authority was closely linked to the concept of *Dharma*. It was righteousness or *Dharma* that truly legitimized the authority of the king. If king failed to hold fast to the path of *dharma* he might suffer adverse consequences. Once the king lost legitimacy, there was possibility of the people changing their opinion about him.

In ancient Indian political thought, the theory of social contract of origin of kingshi played an important role in the constitution of political authority. The roots of social contract theory could be traced back to the Vedic literature when Indra was elected as the king of gods to fight against the demons. It is to the credit of Dr. U. N. Ghoshal that he has found the mention of the contract in the *Brahmana* literature. In the *Brahmana* literature, there is a reference to voluntary agreement between gods to consolidate themselves in a political society. *Tanunapatra* meant 'covenant made by the sacrificer and the priests in the name of (god) Tanunapat not to injure one another.' (Ghoshal, 1966: 29-30) In the ceremony of *Tanunapatra*, political authority was created when voluntarily people decided to surrender their rights and vowed to follow the covenant of not injuring each other. One can say that this was the beginning of theory of social contract which was subsequently developed by the *arthashastra- Smriti* tradition.

There were mainly three theories of social contract. In the Buddhist theory, *Mahasammata* was elected to protect the life and property of the people. In the *arthashastra- Smriti* theory of social contract, along with the contract of reciprocal relationship between the king and the subjects, there is a mention of divine intervention. He was not elected by the people but he was sent by God and the people had an agreement with him. King Manu feared that he would incur sin if he punished the wrong doers. In politics, you had to use force and violence to bring the people under the control. Those people who sought pursuit of *dharma* through truth and non-violence did not want to get involved in politics. Manu initially did not want to accept sovereignty because of this only. He was promised by the people that they would share the sin of violence that the king had to use against wrong doers. In the case of Kapavya, he laid down certain conditions to the people of his tribe which included abandoning some of their old practices, so that new kingship could be properly established.

There are three theories to legitimise authority of the state. The first theory was that of divine origin of kingship with an elaborate ritual of consecration ceremony which invested divine attributes in the king. The second theory was that of social contract which justified regular obedience of the royal order. The third theory was that of righteousness which flew from the office of the king. It is pointed out by Dr. Coomarswami that in the *Rajasuya*, the king's 'divinity' was not 'his own', not 'this man's' who sat upon the throne, but that of the principle that over ruled him and of which he was, not the reality, but the living image, instrument and puppet. (Coomarswami, 1978: 84) This righteousness was acquired by establishing peace in the soul of the king. The king who departed from the path of righteousness was bound to lose his kingdom even if he was a lord of whole earth. Therefore, Kautilya said that a weak but a righteous king was more powerful than a strong and a wicked king because the people rallied behind him at the time of emergency.

But the dominant theme of Indian political theory of authority was that it was based on social contract and the real peace prevailed in the state when both the parties followed the terms of contract.

But at the same time, the principle of righteousness was also pressed in service to give it moral sanction.

Forms of Political Protest in Ancient India

In the Indian tradition, the people followed different forms of protest against the established authority. Indians imbibed the principle of fearlessness or *abhayatva* which was the hallmark of *Dharma.* Therefore, a young girl, a prostitute and an old woman challenged the authority of the wicked king which led to his ouster. The girl climbed the back of the elephant to admonish the king. Similarly a leather worker refused to give his land for construction of temple to the king because the king did not follow proper procedure. As a result, the king had to come to his house to request for the land. These two incidents from the *Katha Sarit Sagar* and the *Rajatarangini* clearly showed that the Indian people possessed courage to challenge the authority of the king.

In the *Jataka* stories, in the stories of the *Katha Sarit Sagar* and the historical account of the *Rajatarangini*, there is a continuity of forms of protest that people used. Despite the existence of some good kings, there were a number of evil kings who became slaves of passion, lost control over their senses and became covetous. At times, they became instruments in the hands of their evil ministers. In all the three texts, it is the people who killed many of them in mass action or they became the victims of intrepid assassins or they died due to diseases or due to divine intervention! Wicked kings were consumed by their own misdeeds. There is no case where a wicked tyrant enjoyed life as in the moment of success also, he remained unsure of himself and his life. Street demonstrations and the mob violence were the methods used by the people to express their resentment against the kings.

In the *Rajatarangini* Kalhana gave us information about the hunger strikes by Brahmins in protest against the anti-people and vicious policies of the kings. In the *Katha Sarit Sagar*, there was a case of a Brahmin and his wife committing suicide to protest against the unjust order passed by the sheriff of the city. The Ramayana mentioned that the Brahmins offered dharanas and obstructed traffic to protest. But hunger strike as a form of political protest was first time used in Kashmir Kings feared hunger strikes by Brahmins because they opened up the gate for political rebellions against them. Many of political revolutions of Kashmir had a background of hunger strikes. These hunger strikes caused death of a good number of Brahmins. Extremely wicked kings like Jayapida or Harsha allowed them to die but other sensible kings took remedial steps to satisfy them. These fasts added fuel to the ongoing agitations. Brahmins also took recourse to hunger strike to bring about reconciliation between king Ananta and his son Kalasha. But all hunger strikes were not motivated by public interest only as some times, fasting Brahmins took political sides and undertook hunger strike to embarrass the king or to add fuel to fire of resentment against the king. Sometimes hunger strikes gave birth to revolts against the kings. On few occasions, they were undertaken to have bribes from both the parties. A Kashmir general Tunga understood this aspect of the hunger strike and used the methods of bribery, dissention and force to break the hunger strikes against him.

Hunger strike was a peaceful method of protest in which supreme self-sacrifice was made to change the unjust policies of the government or to overthrow the regime of an unjust king. Sometimes the armed groups used violence to effect change in the government by driving away the tyrant. On many occasions, the kings themselves decided to abdicate the throne and retired to jungle. Some of them were lynched by the angry mobs. Sometimes they were assassinated by their sons or ministers or poisoned by the people who were close to him. Thus, many kings met violent death.

In the '*Rajatarangini*' there was a case of moral heroism of Vijayraj who decided to kill the evil minister when more than 90 Brahmins committed suicide to protest the unjust policies of the minister. He told his brother that he was killing him because that would enhance the cause of Dharma and save lives of many people. He was killing the minister because sometimes the evil had to be destroyed because a great apostle of non-violence Jina also killed a dragon to save the lives of living beings. After attacking the minister Vijayraj did not run away from the scene and fearlessly told the king that he had killed the minister. He could have very well run away from the scene. But like a Chadrashekhar Azad, he stood his ground and laid down his life giving tough fight to the soldiers of the king. The Geeta inspired him. Perhaps, he thought that killing a tyrant was a divine mission that he had to perform. The God had made him an instrument to fulfill the mission. It was the promise of Lord Krishna that to save good people, to kill the wicked and to establish righteousness, he would take birth. The Geeta's message was heard by Vijayraj as well as by many armed revolutionaries like Madanlal Dhingra and Khudiram Bose. The assassination was not undertaken as an act of personal revenge or to capture political power or to show one's own bravery but it was undertaken to save the lives of many innocent people, to punish the unrighteous minister and to extend help to the good people. Thus, it was a moral heroism which had no parallel in medieval Indian history and the self-less young revolutionaries of modern India could very well be called his successors.

Vijayraj was a hero as well as an ideologue because he put forward his own ideology of protest.

In the *Mahabharata* and the *Jatakas*, there were many instances of political protest and mass action and due to that political change was brought about in several states. In this action, the people from the urban and the rural areas took part. One of the important aspects of succession was that the successor was unanimously chosen by the people and many a times, he was an outsider. This was done to prevent any section of a political group which was opposed to the deposed king to capture power because that might give birth to old animosities. In the *Rajatarangini,* when one group of the party captured power, other group tried to destabilise its power because the rivalry intensified animosities among the people. Even Krishna faced same problem in the Andhaka-Vrishni-Samgha and always feared internal revolts. (Mahabharata, 12.82)

In the *arthashastra* of Kautilya, the issue of political protest and revolt is tackled from different angle. His position was a statist position as he viewed rebellions as calamity befalling the state. But he warned kings that they would have to face the rebellions if they did not control their senses and behaved unjustly. He gave the instances of Kamsa and the Haihaya Arjuna. Therefore, he did not favour despoism and warned king that they had to suffer consequences of their evil behaviour. He correctly defined the term revolt as *kopa* or wrath of the people. The people became angry when they changed their opinion about the ruler. When there was the change of opinion in the minds of our own people, the revolt took place. He had also discussed the causes of rebellion as well as the people who took part in it. The revolts took place in the interior as well as in the outer regions and the revolts taking place in the interior were more dangerous and they were as dangerous as a snake hidden in the bedroom! On the whole he did not favour regicide. King Lalitaditya echoed views of Kautilya when he said that the people living in the rural areas shouldn't be allowed to retain surplus in their hands as this could lead them to sedition. Kautilya said that in the newly settled crown areas, the king should exact maximum work from the cultivators and social gatherings in these areas should not be allowed because they could become breeding grounds of political disaffection. (Chousalkar, 1991: 53) Though Kautilya did not justify political protests of the people but he was realistic enough to understand that such protests and revolts were inevitable if the kings turned tyrants, didn't exercise self-control and disregarded their duties.

The *Katha Sarit Sagar* and the *Rajatarangini* represented different period and they were more enthusiastic about the revolts of the people because they did not approve of tyranny. They knew evil consequences of anarchy but they thought that dread of anarchy was no justification for allowing the wicked kings to rule. Thus, their approach was more consistent with that of the *Mahabharata* than that of the *arthashastra* of Kautilya.

Ideology of Reconciliation in Ancient India

The ideology of revolt and protest was justified in the Vedic as well as in the Buddhist literature. In the Vedic literature, the rule by despot was not appreciated and there were examples of bad kings such being expelled from the kingdom. Vedic literature and the *Mahabharata* constantly laid stress upon the fact that the king had to continuously follow the righteous policies and he should merge his own self-interest in the interest of the people. We have examples of great *Rajarshis* of the past who succeeded in governing the state in the cause of the people and in the spirit of detachment.

In the *Mahabharata*, the principle of fearlessness was considered as an important aspect of *Dharma* and the person who oppressed others for his self-interest was called a wolf in human form. Bhishma in the *Anushasana parva* advocated the killing of tyrannical king by the people like a mad dog. In the *Jatakas*, the *Panchatantra*, the *Katha Sarit Sagar* and the *Rajatarangini* we had several examples of lynching of the kings by the people. Ideological justification for such killing was based on the concept of *Dharma* as sage Vamadeva in the *Shantiparva* of the *Mahabharata* clearly said that such a tyrant got perished along with his family and kinsmen because he followed the path of unrighteousness. In the Geeta, it was clearly said that in the event of emergency when the life of the people had become unbearable, he himself would appear in the world and destroy the evil doers. Even modern revolutionaries drew inspiration from this statement of Lord Krishna.

Second ideological justification was provided by the Buddhist ethics. Both the *Katha Sarit Sagar* and the *Rajatarangini* were influenced by the Buddhist ethics. It was their firm belief that the path of the Buddha was the path of peace, compassion and reconciliation. The Bodhisattva did not believe in his own personal salvation as he was trying to achieve salvation for mankind. He didn't want to return evil for the evil but he wanted to return good for the evil in the hope that the evil would disappear. Ideologically, Buddha showed an alternative path of development as he opposed the Vedic sacrifices, Varna system and violence involved in the superstitious rituals. But along with this ideological opposition, he put forward an alternative path of progress. He gave positive alternative. There are two instances of this. In the story of Magha, there was a clear indication of an alternative path. Magha took the help of 30 colleagues and continuously worked for the welfare of the people by constructing roads, bridges, rest houses and hospitals for them. He showed the right path by performing his righteous duties in the spirit of detachment as he did not want any returns for the same. He was opposed by the corrupt village chief and on his complaint, the king gave orders to execute them without making any inquiry. Magha told his colleagues that they should continue to maintain feeling of friendship and love towards the village chief, the king and the elephant which was brought to crush them. The elephant refused to crush them. The king made inquiries in the province and he came to know that Magha and his friends had effected great change in the area and the people were living happily. There were no court cases as there was no theft or personal quarrels and peace prevailed. The king wanted to execute the corrupt village chief but Magha requested the king to give him, reprieve. He said : "Due to this village chief only, we could meet you and our principles were tested on the crucible of Dhamma, (Kosambi, 2007: 37)

In the Kootdanta Sutra, Buddha preached that instead of performing the costly sacrifices that took lives of great many animals and that made slaves and the workers were forced to hara toil; the king should follow an alternative path of development. Performance of sacrifices was no answer to growing law and order problem in the state. He had to give land, seeds, cattle and monetary support to the people who had taken to robbery due to their poverty. The king should stop sacrifices and follow the path of development which would greatly help the people.

Another important aspect of Buddha's path was tolerance and ability to synthesise one's own viewpoint with the traditional viewpoint. After achieving prosperity, the king wanted to perform sacrifice. Buddha allowed him to do so by laying down three conditions :

(1) He should take the consent of the people

(2) He should follow the principle of non-violence and sacrifice no animal in the Yajnya.

(3) He should do not give or accept any gifts in the function and people should use that money for constructing roads wells and rest houses.

This was Buddha's revolutionary method of bringing about the change from within. As a result, slowly nature of sacrifice changed and subsequently in the *Mahabharata*, it was said that Yajnya stood for sacrifice and purification of one's own soul.

Buddha had developed his own theory of political resistance as he had asked the people not to tolerate injustice. When he was young, he did not support the decision of the Shakya assembly to wage a war against the Koliyas. He was in minority and the decision in favour of the war was taken. He said that he would not support the decision of the majority and in consequence of that he was ready to leave the kingdom. (Ambedkar, 1992: 11-24)

Buddha made it clear that one who deserved punishment must be punished because it was the result of his action. He should harbour no ill will but showing of love and undergoing punishment would purify his soul. He shouldn't lament his fate but rejoice at it. Buddha was opposed to warfare that did injury to the brother but he did not blame these people who made all possible efforts to preserve peace but failed to do so. Their struggle in favour of the righteous cause was not blame worthy. Buddha said that he taught surrender of self but he did not teach surrender to the evil. Man should struggle but shouldn't struggle for self-interest but for the sake of truth and righteousness. One who fought for personal glory or self-aggrandisement would get no rewards but one who fought in the cause of truth and morality would get rewards and even his defeat would be considered as victory. Buddha said that one who had gone for a battle in the righteous cause must always be ready for the supreme sacrifice and he should have no complaints. But the one who had secured victory, should shed hatred and ill-will and lift his defeated foe up and say. "Come now and make peace and let us be brothers." If he accepted his request he would gain victory and as well as rewards. He told Simha the chief of the Licchani Samgha. "Struggle then, Oh! general, courageously; and fight your battles vigorously but be a soldier of truth and the Tathgata will bless you." (Carus, 1972: 125-29)

In the Mahabharata it is said that the esstence of dharma was fearlessness. The great epic said that the people should not get afraid of thieves, kings and the wicked people and they should imbibe principle of fearlessness or abyayatva.

Ancient Indian thinkers believed in effecting change in the heart by following the method of self-sacrifice because they thought that its impact would be long lasting. King Jimutavahana was influenced by the Buddhist ethics, hence, he decided to offer himself as a victim of Garuda to save the life of innocent Naga youth. This self-sacrifice brought change of heart and the Garuda decided to end enmity with the Nagas. Similarly, the Kashmir king Meghavahana was ready to offer his own life to save the life of the child. He believed that the righteous behaviour was good for its own sake. Great kings in the *Katha Sarit Sagara* and the *Rajatarangini* held that there was no escape from the evil but the best way to deal with it was not to return the evil but to return the good to the evil because that would ultimately reduce the impact of the evil. Therefore, they urged kings to remain steadfast on the path of *dharma* and do not fall prey to the policy of 'tit for tat' or '*Shathe Prati Shathyam.*'

Thus, the Indians in ancient India mainly followed different forms of protest. First, they staked their lives against injustice and committed suicide. Secondly, there were mass agitations, dharanas and demonstrations by the people as a form of protest to show their disaffection. In many cases, the kings either ran away or abdicated the throne. Thirdly, the Brahmins in Kashmir undertook the hunger strikes and fasts against the tyrant to exert pressure on the government. Many of them died because of the fast. Fourthly, people came together, became violent and lynched the tyrants. Fifthly, wicked king or wicked minister were killed by young revolutionary. Sixthly and lastly, ruling dynasties and kings were removed from power by their ambitious rivals; taking advantage of disaffection of the people and anti-government hunger strikes by the Brahmins.

Relevance in Modern India

India came under the British rule in the first two decades of nineteenth century and the Indians fought one of the most non-violent freedom struggles against them. Great Indian leaders like Shri Aurobindo, Lokmanya Tilak and Mahatma Gandhi developed the theory of political resistance which was based on passive resistance and non-violence. They wrote commentaries on the Bhagvat Geeta to justify their political action.

It is rightly pointed out by Dharampal that the Indians continued to follow their traditional methods of protest against the British rulers in the first decade of nineteenth century but they were suppressed by the Britishers using the brute force. Their methods were largely peaceful. After these failures the subaltern sections in Western India and Bihar and Bengal rose but their violent movements were suppressed. After 1885, the educated Indians decided to follow new methods of protest and the new method was based on mass mobilisation of the people. There was a group of leaders who decided to launch armed struggle.

Mahatma Gandhi developed his theory of Satyagraha to fight the foreign government. He largely followed the Buddhist ethic which laid stress upon purity of means. Gandhi borrowed five important principles from the tradition and they were as follows:

(1) Fearlessness

(2) Organising dharanas and demonstrations of the people.

(3) Hunger strike or fast unto death to press for demands.

(4) Non-violence and lack of ill-will towards the enemy.

(5) Constructive programme as the other side of Satyagraha.

It is rightly said that Gandhi wanted to bring about change in the heart of enemy and he never nursed any ill will. He did not want to secure any political benefit out of his struggle.

Gandhi creatively used the method of fasting and unlike the Brahmains of Kashmir, he did not issue the threat of suicide. Kalhan did not give any moral justification of hunger strikes by Brahmins. They must have developed it in the course of action. In the Vedic texts, the Jatakas, the Mahabharata and in other texts it is argued that ultimately legitimacy of king is based on his commitment to Dharma if he deviated from it he was bound to lose his authority to rule. Modern Indian political thinkers also laid stress upon the importance of morality and purity of means. They agreed with the ancient thinkers that non-violence and fearlessness flew from the concept of Dharma.

In the revolutionary armed struggle, there was always discussion on the desirability of use of arms and assassinations. In Vijayraj we could see the representative of modern Indian revolutionaries. He justified the assassination of wicked minister on moral grounds and held that in exceptional circumstances, we had to take recourse to violent means. Like Bhagt Singh, he did not leave the place and like Chandrashekhar Azad, he died fighting against king's soldiers and like Khudiram Bose he swore by the Geeta.

During the British rule and after independence also the Indians continued to use these methods of protest against the government. Gandhi used his unique method of Satyagraha to secure independence of the country by non-violent means. Indians continued to use the method of hunger strikes and fasting to get their grievances redressed. Many upper caste students protesting against the implementation of recommendations of the Mandal Commission committed suicides. These suicides destroyed political career of the then Prime minister V.P. Singh. Social activists like Jai Prakash Narayana, Dr. Ram Manohar Lohia, Medha Patkar, Sundarlal Bahuguna and Anna Hazare also followed different methods of protest to press for their demands.

One of the major changes in modern times is that now we can change the governments by voting them out of power. In ancient times the method of the periodic elections was not there, therefore, the people had to use violent means.

References

Ambedkar, B. R. (1994), The Writings and the Speeches of Dr. B.R. Ambedkar, Vol. XI, *Buddha and His Dhamma*, Government of Maharashtra, Mumbai.

Carus, P. (1992), *Gospel of Buddha*, Omen Communications, Tucson.

Chousalkar, A. (1991), *A Comparative Study of Theory of Rebellion in Aristotle and Kautilya,* Indological Book House, Delhi.

Coomarswami, A. (1978), *The Spiritual Authority and the Temporal power in the Indian Theory of Government*, Motilal Banarassidass, Delhi.

Ghoshal U. N. (1966), *A History of Indian Political Ideas*, Oxford University Press.

Kosambi, Dharmanand (2002), *Buddha-Leela*, Government of Maharashtra, Mumbai.

Conclusion

The problem of constitution of political authority and various forms of protest that the people used against the state is the central problem of political theory. It defined the relationship between the state and the people. In any civilised political system, there has to have proper development of methods of political protest if the political authority is wrongly used by the people who hold it. The protests are symptom of the disease that affected the body politic and perhaps they work as some sort of medicine to purify the system. It is not possible for the people to endure the tyrannical government for a period of long duration.

In this study, an attempt is made to examine critically the political authority and forms of political protest in Indian tradition. It is contended by some scholars on history of India who were under the influence of the Orientalist historiography that Indian state was a despotic state and the people lived under the perpetual slavery of these despots. Thus, there was a system of Oriental despotism. Now it is true that monarchy was a normal form of government in ancient India during the Christian era but all monarchs were not tyrants. Many of them were enlightened kings. In Europe's history also, situation is not different and compared to the oriental despots, the European despots were more violent and more vicious. We have shown in our study of constitution of political authority and forms of political protest in ancient India that political authority in India was not that despotic and Indians visualised the social contract as the basis of the authority. The *Smriti* tradition held that the king was a servant of the people and taxes paid by the people was his salary for the work he discharged. Indian people were fearless and they used numerous methods of protest against the tyranny of the king or his minister. Thus, they were not docile spectators but they were actual participants in the affairs of the state. Hence, the role of Paura and Janapada- principal elements from the urban and rural areas is constantly mentioned in all the texts on ancient Indian polity.

The Indian tradition constantly mentioned the fact that exercise of *Danda* or political authority is a very difficult art and the maximum care has to be taken because it has to be used in consonance with principle of *Dharma*. The king has to imbibe the principles of *Dharma* in his behaviour. He has to first establish Swaraj or self-government in his soul so that he could establish it in his kingdom. If the king became a slave of passions and out of covetousness and greed if he started harassment of the subjects, the texts point out that he would meet his nemesis sooner than later. The *Jataka*s, the *Mahabharata* and other texts cite numerous examples to show that such despots were overthrown by the people or they were driven out from the kingdom.

Social contract theory and consecration of the king were two principal instruments of legitimising the authority of the state. Social contract theory justified the right of the king to issue orders and the duty of the people to obey them. The ritual of consecration poured moral and religious meaning in it so that its universal character can be properly appreciated. These two bases provide durable legitimacy to political authority.

Acharya Vinoba Bhave had described four methods of resistence which were as follows:

(1) Resist with greater violence,

(2) Resist with equal violence,

(3) Resist with non-violence,

(4) Resist not evil but carry out constructive activities. (Bhave, V, 1999: 130-31)

He is of the view that first method was followed by the politicians who used greater force to defeat the evil as they wanted to capture political power. The second method was followed by the Jew prophet

Mozes who believed in the theory of retribution. He stood for an eye for an eye. Third method was followed by Tolstoy and Gandhi who tried to resist injustice with non-violent means. Fourth method was not openly resisting injustice but at the same time, it believed in carrying out constructive activities which would remove the causc of injustice Vinoba's Bhoodan movement was launched in Telangana to stem agrarian violence born out of the land question.

In Ancient India, many rebels who wanted to capture political power by overthrowing the rule of the king followed first method and used greater violence of enraged mobs to kill or drive away the king. Second method of using equal violence was followed to discipline the errant king. The third method was used by Brahmins in Kashmir as they launched the hunger strikes against wrong policies of the king. The fasts were non-violent in nature but there was threat of committing suicide if demands were not met. Gandhi did not give threat of suicide to king because he did not approve the use of suicide as a political weapon. The fourth method was followed by Magha who performed constructive activities in the background of unjust behaviour of the village chief.

Buddha provided the ideological basis to the various forms of protest used by the Indian people. He exercised strong influence on the *Jatakas*, the *Shantiparva*, the *Katha Sarit Sagar* and the *Rajatarangini*. He was of the opinion that we should not surrender to the forces of evil and we should fight against it but in the process, we should try to change it from within by employing the principle of righteousness. The methods of peace and conciliation are the best methods and a victor should use them to win the friendship of his enemy. Buddha was interested in long-term goals of a particular policy and he always wanted to study the consequences of all these actions. Therefore, political philosophy of Gautam Buddha is still relevant today and in modern India, Mahatma Gandhi used some of the ideas and methods during India's independence movement. He held that his Satyagraha was launched to purify one's own soul and to transform the heart of the opponent. Struggle launched in the cause of truth and righteousness would always bring good results. Thus, the methods and principles suggested by Buddha and Bhishma are still relevant today. The ancient Indian methods of reconciliation and resolution of conflict need to be emulated in India because at present, Indian society is adversely affected by the Western style of competitive politics and competitive market system that intensify contradictions and encourage conflicts. It is necessary to relearn some of the methods of ancient Indian people how to reconcile the contradictions and how to resolve the conflicts by pursuing the process of assimilation. Buddha did not believe in confrontation as well as in meek surrender to evil. He always wanted to open up new avenues of dialogue therefore, he did not develop moral indignation against the sinners as he always hoped that they could be improved. In the *Rajatarangini*, it was said that the Bodhisattvas did not want to achieve salvation for themselves but they want to achieve salvation for entire mankind and for that purpose they were willing to suffer in day-to-day life but they would not return in the jungle in pursuit of personal salvation.

History of Kashmir is history of conflicts and wars but the common people developed the method of hunger strikes against the oppressive rulers. It is an important innovation which is continuously followed by the Indian people. This fearlessness of the Indian people was suppressed by the British rulers. Indians continued to follow these methods of protest upto early decades of nineteenth century and it was Gandhi who revived fearlessness of Indian people. (Dharam Pal, 1971: 9-15) Waging struggles against injustice but at the same time, leaving scope for reconciliation was the essence of Indian method of political resistance.

Social contract was the basis of political authority but ultimately political authority of any king was based on his performance in the office. The king could spoil the mandate if he became the slave of passions and covetous. We have several examples from the history of Kashmir that even good kings spoiled their careers because of excessive love of wealth and sensuous pleasures. In the *arthashastra-Smriti* tradition it was constantly argued that the king was maintained by the people by paying him the salary in the form of taxes because he protected them. The king had to display higher power of governance but at a times the temporal power could develop temptation to use might against the right and in consequence, the order got disturbed. Hence, the rulers had to hold fast to the path of righteousness.

During the Vedic and the post-Vedic period the sacrificial rituals played an important role. The kings performed the *Sautramani* sacrifice to win back the favour of the people. But with the decline in the influence of the *Atharvan* practices. secularisation of politics, kings no longer thought it necessary to perform the *sautramani* sacrifice but the impact of the religious was strong. The Indian political theory of government, believed in the unity of spiritual authority and temporal power. It is argued by Dr. Coomarswami that "The essence of traditional politics amounts to this that 'self-government' (Swaraj) depends upon self-control (Atma Samyam), rule on unruliness. One may say that this conception of government survives even in modern India, since the political victory foreseen by Gandhi is assuredly one that can only be achieved by a self-conquest." (Coomarswami, 1978: 85).

References

Bhave, V., *Lokniti*, Parandham Prakashan, Wardha, 1998. Coomar Swami A. T., *Spiritual Power and Temporal Power in the Indian Theory of Government*, Motilal Banarasidass, Delhi.

Dharam Pal (1971), *Civil Disobedience in Indian Tradition*, Other India Book Store, Goa.

Bibliography

(A) Primary Sources:

Aitereya Brahmana, translated by A. B. Keith, Horward Oriental Series, Vol. XXV, 1920.

The Atharvaveda Samhita translated by R.T.H. Griffith, Banaras, 1987.

The Atharvaveda Marathi translation by N. G. Chapekar.

The Ramayana, Vol. III. Varada, Pune.

Rigveda Samhita translated by R.T.H. Griffith, 1886-97.

_________ translated by F. Geldner, Horward Oriental Series, Vols. XXXIII-XXXIV, 1951.

_________ critical edition, 5 volumes, Vedic Samshodhan Mandal, Pune.

_________ Marathi translation, Siddheshvar Shastri Chitrav, Vedic Vangmaya Samshodhan Mandal, Pune, 1938.

_________ *Srutibodha*- Marathi translation of the *Rigveda*, by R.V. Patvardhan, S.M. Joshi and Brothers, Pune, 1928.

The Jatakas in 7 volumes edited by E.B. Cowell, Cambridge, 1995-183.

The Siddhartha Jataka in 7 volumes, translated in Marathi by Durga Bhagavat, Varada Publications, Pune, 2000-2001.

Diga Nikaya edited by T.W. Rhys Davids and J.E. Carpenter, 3 volumes, Pali Text Society, 1980, 1903, 1911.

Digha Nikaya Marathi translation C. V. Rajwade in three volumes, Sayaji Oriental Series, Baroda, 1936-37.

The Mahabharata – Critical edition, Vols. 1-5, Bhandarkar Oriental Research Institute, Pune, 1977.

_________ with commentary by Neelkantha, edited by R. Kinjavadekar, Pune, 1929-33.

_________ translated in English by M.N. Dutt, H.C. Dass, Calcutta, 1895-1905.

_________ Marathi translation by A. Rashivadekar and others, Chiploonkar and Mandali, Varada, Pune, 2000.

The Arthashastra of Kautilya in three volumes, Pune, Text and translation by R. P. Kangle, University of Mumbai, Mumbai 1974-75.

_________ Marathi translation by R. P. Kangle, Government of Maharashtra, Mumbai, 1985.

_________ English translation by R. Shama-Shastri, Mysore, 1929.

The Katha Sarit Sagar translated in Marathi in 5 volumes, Durga Bhagavat Varada, Pune, 2002.

The Ocean of Stories in 10 volumes by Penzer, Sawyar, London, 1929.

The Rajatarangini by Kalhana, edited by M. A. Stein, Bombay-1882 translated by Stein, Westminster, 1900.

_________ translated by Ranjit Pandit Sahitya Akademy, Delhi, 2002.

The *Panchatantra* translated by A. Ryder. Jaico, Mumbai, 1971.

The Shataka Trayi of Bhartihari edited by D. Kosambi, Varada, Pune, 1996.

(B) Secondary Books:

Agravala, V.S., *India as Known to Panini* (Second edition), Prithvi, Varanasi, 1963.

_________, *The Bharat Savitri,* in three volumes, Sasta Sahitya, Delhi, 1966.

Altekar, A. S., *The State and Government in Ancient India*, Motilal Banarassidas, Delhi, 1971.

Anjaria, J. J., *Nature and Grounds of Political Obligation in the Hindu State,* Longmans Green and Co., London, 1935.

Banerjee, S. C., *Smriti Material in the Mahabharata* Benerjee, Calcutta, 1972.

Basham, A. L., *History and Doctrines of the Ajivikas*, Motilal Banarassidas, Delhi, 2002.

_________, *The Wonder that was India*, Orient Longman, Bombay, 1963.

Basu, J., *India of the Age of the Brahmanas*, Sanskrit Pustak Bhandar, Calcutta, 1969.

Bhattacharya, S., *Secular and Pluralistic elements in the idea of State in early India*, Indian Institute of Advanced Study, Shimla, 2002.

Carus, P., *Gospel of Buddha*, TUSCON Omen, 1972.

Chousalkar, A., *Social and Political Implications of Concepts of Justice and Dharma*, Mittal, Delhi, 1986.

_________, *A Comparative Study of Theory of Rebellion in Kautilya and Aristotle,* Indological Book House, Delhi, 1991.

Coomarswami, A. K., *The Spiritual Authority and Temporal power in the Indian Theory of Government,* Munshiram Manoharlal, Delhi, 1978.

De Barry (Ed.), *Sources of Indian Tradition*, Motilal Banarassidas, Delhi, 1977.

Drekmeier, C., *Kingship and Community in Early India*, Oxford University Press, Bombay, 1962.

Ganguli, N. C., *Indian Political Philosophy*, Kamala Book Depot, Calcutta, 1939.

Ghoshal, U.N., *A History of Indian Political Ideas,* Oxford University Press, Mumbai, 1966.

Heesterman, J. C., *Ancient Indian Royal Consecration*, Mouton and Co., The Hague, 1957.

__________, *Inner Conflict of the Tradition*, Oxford University Press, Delhi, 1983.

Jayaswal, K. P., *Hindu Polity*, Bangalore Press, Bangalore, 1942.

Jauhari, M., *Ethics and Politics in Ancient India*, Bharatiya Vidya, Varanasi, 1968.

Kane, P. V., *A History of Dharmashastras* in 5 volumes, Bhandarkar Oriental Research Institute, Pune, 1930-72.

Kangle, R. P., *Prachin Bharatiya Rajaniti,* Mauj, Mumbai, 1969.

Kosambi, Dharmanand, *Buddha Leela,* Government of Maharashtra, Mumbai, 2004.

Kosambi, D.D., *An Introduction to the Study of Indian History,* Popular, Mumbai, 1976.

__________, *The Culture and Civilisation of Ancient India*, Vikas, Mumbai, 1975.

__________, *History and Society – Problems of Interpretation*, University of Mumbai, 1985.

Kosambi, Dharmanand (2007), Buddhaleela, Maharashtra Sahitya and Sanskriti Mandal, Mumbai.

Kosambi, Dharmanand (2007), Jataka Katha Sangrah, Maharashtra Sahitya and Sanskriti Mandal, Mumbai.

Malik, S. C. (Ed.), *Dissent Protest and Reform in Indian Tradition,* Indian Institute of Advanced Study, Shimla, 1977.

Meer, G. T., *Dharma and Society*, Luzac and Co., London, 1936.

More, S., *Krishna: Life and Mission,* Gaaj Publications, Ahmednagar, 1995.

Mishra, S., *The Janapada States in Ancient India*, Bharatiya Vidya, Varanasi, 1973.

Pandey, U. K., *Political Concepts and Institutions in the Shukla Yajurveda*, Janaki, Patna, 1972.

Rai, Jaimal, *Rural-Urban Economy and Social Change in Ancient India*, Bharatiya Vidya, Varanasi, 1973.

Roychoudhuri, H. C., *Political History of Ancient India,* University of Calcutta, Calcutta, 1950.

Ruben, W., *Studies in Ancient Indian Thought*, Indian Studies, Calcutta, 1966.

Saletore, B. A. (1971), Political ideas and Institutions in Ancient India, Bombay, Asia Publishing House.

Sharma, R. S., *Indian Feudalism*, MacMillan (Third edition), New Delhi, 2006.

__________, *Origin of State in Ancient India*, Department of History, University of Mumbai, 1985.

Spellman, J. C., *Political Theory in Ancient India,* Oxford at Clarendon Press, 1964.

__________, *Some Aspects of Ancient Indian Political Ideas and Institutions*, Motilal Banarassidas, Delhi, 1968.

Thapar, A., *Asoka and Decline of the Mauryas,* Oxford University Press, Delhi, 1973.

__________, *The Cultural Pasts*, Oxford University Press, 2002.

__________, *Ancient Indian Social History,* Orient Longman, Delhi, 1978.

__________, *From Lineage to State*, Oxford University Press, 1983.

Vaidya, C. V., *Epic India*, Gaekwad's Oriental Series, Baroda, 1932.

__________, *History of Medieval India* in three volumes (reprint), Varada, Pune, 2000.

Varma, V. P., *Studies in Hindu Political Thought and Its Metaphysical Foundations*, Munshiram Manoharlal, Agra.

Zimmer, H., *Philosophies of India,* Meridian Books, New Delhi, 1957.

(C) Articles:

Brown, J., "Indian and Western Realism", 266-72, *Indian Journal of Political Science,* Vol. 15, 1954.

Chousalkar, A., "The Concept of the Apaddharma and Moral Dilemma of Politics", pp. 115-27, *Indian Literature*, No. 225.

__________, Power, Authority and legitimacy ancient India, pp. 56-70, Political Science Review Vol.

Ingalls, D. H., "Law and Authority in Ancient India" 35-45, *Journal of American Oriental Society*, Vol. 74, 1954.

Ruben, W., "Fighting Against the Despots in Ancient India", pp. 111-18, *Annals of Bhandarkar Oriental Research Institute*, Vol. 50, 1968.

Index

B

C

D

S

W

Y